T0098544

RED, WHITE, AND LATINA

RED, WHITE, AND LATINA

OUR AMERICAN IDENTITY

CRISTINA PEREZ

NEW YORK

NASHVILLE • MELBOURNE • VANCOUVER

RED, WHITE, AND LATINA
OUR AMERICAN IDENTITY

© 2017 **CRISTINA PEREZ**

All rights reserved. No portion of this book may be reproduced, stored in a retrieval system, or transmitted in any form or by any means—electronic, mechanical, photocopy, recording, scanning, or other,—except for brief quotations in critical reviews or articles, without the prior written permission of the publisher.

Published in New York, New York, by Morgan James Publishing. Morgan James is a trademark of Morgan James, LLC. www.MorganJamesPublishing.com

The Morgan James Speakers Group can bring authors to your live event. For more information or to book an event visit The Morgan James Speakers Group at www.TheMorganJamesSpeakersGroup.com.

ISBN 978-1-68350-443-6 paperback
ISBN 978-1-68350-444-3 eBook
Library of Congress Control Number: 2017901695

Cover Design by:
Ian Koviak
BookDesigners.com

Interior Design by:
Bonnie Bushman
The Whole Caboodle Graphic Design

In an effort to support local communities, raise awareness and funds, Morgan James Publishing donates a percentage of all book sales for the life of each book to Habitat for Humanity Peninsula and Greater Williamsburg.

Get involved today! Visit
www.MorganJamesBuilds.com

*For all who believe in the unconditional promise
of America and everything it stands for.*

*And especially to my family, Dario and Aracelly, Claudia, and
Joe – you are the core of my identity and my daily inspiration.*

TABLE OF CONTENTS

THE DEBT WE OWE

Senator Nina Turner

The debt I owe was left to me as a moral obligation by my ancestors, my foremothers, my forefathers and closer to home, it was left by my own family.

My mother was raised in a middle class household, and she was the only child. On paper, my mother could have grown up and been anything that she wanted to be. But everybody doesn't run this race at the same pace. Some people have setbacks that are greater than others, or impediments that stop one person but motivate another. My mother seemingly had it all, but her life took a different turn.

One morning, not unlike any other, I saw my mother before heading off to my classes. It was 1992 and I was 22 years old, a sophomore at Cuyahoga Community College trying to become a cycle-breaker in my family. By that night, I was being told that an aneurysm had burst in her brain and my mother was in a coma. A week or so later I was told that she would never come out of that coma.

My mother died at the age of 42. She died with her dreams deferred, in the words of the poet Langston Hughes from his poem *Harlem*.

She died on the system of welfare. She didn't even have a life insurance policy.

I was 22 years old, a college student, a wife, and had a baby of my own. I was the oldest of 7 children with my baby sister 12 years old. Now, I became the full-fledged "mama," of my family.

My grandmother died 4 months later; my grandmother our matriarch, with only a 3rd grade education. She taught me the principles of: study hard, work hard, and treat people the way that you want to be treated. Those principles never left me, from those early challenges of picking up where my mother left off and raising my family, all the way to my life of political service to our nation today.

Even more than Fannie Lou Hamer, Daisy Bates, Shirley Chisholm and Rosa Parks, all of those well-known, fearless women who made their mark on history. It was the two women who raised me - my grandmother and my mother - who really made their marks on me. It was through their deaths that I was able to muster the strength to become a first generation college graduate. Even though they never lived to see it, I did it in their memory. As a Cleveland City Councilwoman I took the oath of office in their memory. I became a State Senator in their memory. I ran for statewide office in their memory. And in the presidential election of 2016, I was a proud national surrogate for one of the most inspirational presidential candidates in the history of this country, in their memory. All those things, I know that they would be proud of, even though they're not here to see it.

They paved the path for me to be where I am today. I feel personally that I owe them that I owe their spirit, I owe everything that they stood for, and I owe the people who are still very much alive today who were in the civil rights movement. I certainly owe my ancestors who have long passed.

I owe them a debt that I can never ever repay. But I also owe a down payment on that debt. And the down payment on that debt, in the words of Shirley Chisholm, is service, the rent we pay to be here on this earth.

The author you're about to meet in these pages, Cristina Perez, also understands this debt we all owe as Americans. In fact, she has a deep understanding of every core principle I have just written about, from our shared concern about the tears in the fabric of our national identity to the legacy this discord and drama will leave for future generations.

As the product of immigrant parents, Cristina understands what is at stake in finding, as she says, the "common sense, common values, and common ground," that will reunite our great nation.

On a personal note, I've been a fan of Cristina's courtroom television shows for years. I have a deep admiration of her obvious passion for the letter of the law, the compassion she shows toward her litigants, and the constant integrity with which she carries herself.

Cristina is truly a voice of the people – all people, from all ethnicities, races, social and economic classes, gender identities, religions and political ideologies. She walks with us and speaks for us. I cannot think of a more qualified person to raise and explore the extremely important issues in this book, the very ones dividing America.

I am honored to now introduce to you a fellow mother, wife, public personality, concerned citizen, author, and a unifying voice for a country greatly in need of it - Cristina Perez.

ACKNOWLEDGMENTS

Thank you to…

The American Immigration Council.

My agent Andrew Lear at United Talent Agency.

Michael Maples.

Sabra Miller.

Christine Whitmarsh: What do you say about someone who can finish your thoughts and put them down on paper perfectly? I'm so grateful for our indescribable bond and your ability to so beautifully express what is in my heart.

Adryenn Ashley: You don't just "step up to the plate" you sprint up to it! I'm forever in awe of your quick creativity, contagious energy, and loyalty.

Senator Nina Turner: For contributing your inspiring story and powerful personal identity to this book. I'm so grateful for your contribution!

Jessica Reeder: For your professionalism and attention to detail.

Mike: Not only an American patriot who served our country, but a person who believes in the worth of everything America stands for. Your words and ideas helped create the foundation of this book.

Natalia, Alicia, Genesis and Alejandra: Because of you I can do so much more than I could alone. You are all beautiful and I'm grateful to have you - you're my A team!

David Hancock and the entire team to Morgan James Publishing: For your instant support and enthusiasm for this book.

JoJo: For your selfless loving support.

My husband Chris, my best friend: For making my life anything but boring and for inspiring me every day to become a deeper version of who I am.

My incredibly beautiful and intelligent daughter and contributing book author Sofia: Thank you for making me want to be better, every day. I hope you take from this book that you should always demand more from yourself. You're always more capable than you think you are as long as you give everything 100%, because in life there are no do overs.

Prologue
BULLIES AND BALLOTS

True patriotism springs from a belief in the dignity of the individual, freedom and equality not only for Americans but for all people on earth, universal brotherhood and good will, and a constant and earnest striving toward the principles and ideals on which this country was founded.

—Eleanor Roosevelt

As I sit down to write this book, it is the summer of 2016 in America. The atmosphere hanging over our nation is thick: heavy with anger, violence, distrust, and divisiveness. As a nation, it seems that we are in fear of what's coming next. The election for our 45th president is only four months away, and the party conventions at the epicenter are being shown on all media, in Cleveland and Philadelphia. In the summer of 1968, the streets outside the conventions were on fire. Now, in 2016, the virtual neighborhoods of social media burn with intense emotion.

The threads, spinning down like spiderwebs from each politically oriented status update, are laced with poisonous language and verbal daggers. The words are hostile, emotional, vehement, and frankly disrespectful. I'm not fooled for a minute. No high-minded moral or philosophical battles are being won or lost on this field. This is personal, and the worst kind of personal too. Some people seem to be out for blood. The subtext of each polarized argument is essentially: "I'm right, so you're wrong." Case closed. No further questions.

I wonder why we are making it so personal. Are personal attacks simply the path of least intellectual resistance, allowing us to avoid asking ourselves challenging questions? When we resist challenging our own ideas, we remove the opposing side of an issue and avoid the huge, embarrassing risk of being proven wrong (and ending up with a bruised ego). Have you seen the lengths a person will go to protect his or her ego?

There is a percentage of the online population, at this very moment, which is shouting people into submission: bullying and shaming others into agreeing with their beliefs. Bullies naturally get attention through force. People are afraid to challenge them—or else they assume the bullies must know what they're talking about because they're so loud. Social media has spawned a particularly fearless type of loudmouth: the anonymous bully, who becomes braver by the day because of the low probability of ever facing any consequences of his or her words and actions. The audacity of these bullies' actions, quite frankly, is epic.

Political pundits in the media have created job security based upon this aspect of human nature: whoever yells the loudest seems to drown out the opposition and win the debate. Now, the bullies on social media have followed in the pundits' footsteps; unfortunately, their tactic is working just as well in that environment. The louder the social media bullies yell, the harder it is to hear the other side—and after a while, many people will shrug their shoulders, give up, and decide to agree with the bullies rather than working out informed opinions of their own. This can be comforting: the knowledge that we've picked a side, settled on a point of view, and carried on with life. In a way, it's easier to hide behind these bullies and their bullhorns than to express one's own voice.

But once we've picked a side, why stop and listen to the other point of view—when it's so much easier to swim in the calm, comforting waters of what we think we know? We've stopped listening to anything we don't want to hear, anything that is in opposition to our own point of view, or anything that challenges us. We've decided to reject conflicting opinions, seeing them as threats. In order to protect this sense of mental security and moral superiority, we go to battle not only with anonymous strangers, but also with our friends, co-workers, even family members. There are no victors, only victims: all fighting to be heard, but in the worst possible ways.

Language matters, and some of the terms I'm seeing callously tossed back and forth across the web are downright vile. I am horrified and ashamed, as an American citizen, watching the disrespect shown toward our police, military, lawmakers, powers-that-be, and even all the way to the highest office in the land: the President of the United States.

This is not okay. While the right to free speech gives us the privilege to say these things, it is not a free moral pass that makes it *right* to do so.

When did it become acceptable to hurl the deepest, most personal and heinous insults at our president? From the tone of the conversation between recent presidents and congress, politicians and the media, citizens and police officers, all the way down to how kids speak to their teachers and even their parents—it seems like disrespect is permeating the fabric of American life.

Our children are being affected by the tone of this national conversation. They listen to the words we say and watch the examples we set, absorbing everything and integrating it into their personal identities and future moral compasses. If we parents believe otherwise for one second, we are in complete denial of reality.

Beyond our household walls and national borders, we are also showing the rest of the world what we think of America. While it's true (and this is something I also teach my daughter) that we shouldn't allow the opinions of others to shape who we are, there comes a point when we must consider the consequences of our conversations.

Make no mistake: With the language around this election and other significant national events, we are establishing a new standard of acceptable behavior for future generations of American citizens. Do we want this national conversation to continue on its current path? Where are we going with this?

By the time you read this book, the election will be over and in the history books—and this is *exactly* why we need to continue to have this conversation. If we don't address the problem, if we ignore the fiery division of the 2016 election and the wounds it left behind, they will only continue to fester, and worsen in the years to come. At some point, as a nation, the wounds may become too deep to fully heal. As a proud citizen of this country, that is the fear in my heart. That is why I am writing this book.

I write this for my daughter Sofia, who, with her peers, will grow up in the wake of what we leave behind.

I write for my immigrant parents, who sacrificed everything to move their family here and capture their American Dream, so that theirs and millions of other stories like theirs will not have unfolded in vain.

I write for all the brave soldiers who have died to defend our flag.

I write this book for YOU—for all of us.

I write for the love we all have, no matter how we show it sometimes, of our young but incredibly resilient country.

I write because I am one American voice in a sea of many: an author, an entertainment personality, a daughter of immigrants, a woman, a proud Latina, a wife, and a mother.

My goal is to pose challenging questions that make you reflect on your American identity as an individual, and our identity together as a country. May the questions and answers we all discover together work to redirect our passionate patriotism; may they repair the rift, rebuild the trust, and release the anger that divides us. I hope to see us move forward again toward a bolder, stronger, and more unified future that honors where we came from and celebrates where we are going. Because above all, America stands for an unwavering belief in each citizen's potential: the "what if" that we each have the right to rise up and claim.

It's time to start a common sense, heart-based conversation, one that will help to rebuild our American identity. It begins with a sense of pride in who we are as individuals, where we come from, and the dream we each have for our country.

Introduction

CHALLENGING ASSUMPTIONS

The little girl felt her face burn beet red as her brother and sister teased her about her poor English. The girl knew some words, but was hardly fluent. Her brother and sister were merciless, teasing: "If you live in the United States you need to learn English! They don't speak Spanish in the States!"

The whole family was making the drive over the Mexico-America border, en route to a new life in California. The other children had started quizzing their sister in the car, until she got stumped at how to say *vaca* (cow) in English. After several attempts to remember the translation, and much teasing, the little girl became so frustrated that she finally just yelled: "Mooo!" It was not the right word, but she knew that "moo" was connected with the word for "cow."

"Don't worry, *mija*," the little girl's father tried to reassure her from the front seat. "You will learn."

What kind of assumption would you make about that little girl and her family? Would you assume they were immigrants coming to America in search of opportunity and the American Dream? Or would you see them as a threat to American jobs, and question whether they were crossing the border legally or illegally? Or perhaps a thought would pop into your head about how "those people" are hurting America, and you would see them as a potential danger.

Would it make a difference if you knew I was that little girl? I was born in New York, raised in Mexico as a child, and at the time of this story my family and I were moving back to the United States. Does that change your interpretation of the situation?

There are certain perceptions and assumptions that I have been living with every day of my life. Even though I was born in the US and we re-entered the country legally, my family faced a certain set of negative cultural stereotypes. Most people didn't perceive that my parents were educated, that my father was a doctor, that we were entering the country legally, or anything else that disagreed with their surface assessment of us. They heard the accents, saw where we had arrived from, and put us in a box of assumptions about uneducated, unintelligent, unskilled, untrustworthy strangers from a strange land.

This early reality in my life has forced me to think of my culture ahead of my American citizenship every day. How can I avoid it? It's something I've lived with every single day, as far back as I can remember. I've never had a choice but to think about it, as do a great percentage of Americans.

Let's be honest: when you hear my name, what's the first thing you think about me? You recognize immediately that I am Hispanic/Latina. You see my culture first, then my citizenship. You label me.

I think about being Latina every single day. It defines me as much as being an American does. Whether I'm at work or at home with my family, I speak Spanish as well as English. My name in itself, Cristina Perez Gonzalez, brings with it a whole set of unexpected issues and challenges I have the pleasure of dealing with on a day-to-day basis. (For example, being in "two boxes" gives me the joy of being on English AND Spanish-speaking telemarketing lists!) The fact is, I don't get a "day off" from my cultural identity, nor would I ever want one.

I have pride in my culture. Some people have criticized me for this, implying that it makes me less American. Ironically, I've had people try to convince me: "Oh, you're not Latina, you're American" because maybe it's somehow easier for them if everyone conforms and fits neatly into a single box. These expectations are confusing to me. I shouldn't have to *stop* looking at myself as a Latina woman and only identify myself as American just because others are uncomfortable with the duality of my identity. I don't believe that highlighting my culture makes me somehow unpatriotic.

The facts are: I am Cristina Perez Gonzalez and I was born in the United States, in New York. I am American and my ethnicity is Latina—Colombian to be specific. I will always be labeled as Latina first and then American; so will my daughter, and so will countless other US citizens who happen to be part of a long legacy of immigrants.

How often do you think about *your* culture? There are a few obvious times: for instance, filling out paperwork that asks you to check one or more boxes that best reflect your cultural, racial, and ethnic identity. In a country that blends together so many cultures, that always seems like a strange request to me. Many of us fall into so many different categories. How do we divide ourselves up into little pieces?

Yet the reality is that a large number of American citizens don't know—and will never know—what it's like to be labeled. How can they be expected to understand something that they will never in their lifetime experience? They will never know the feeling of people turning a blind eye to their identity as an American, and seeing only their culture, color, creed, or other labels. For people born into the cultural majority of their country, it's hard to know what that experience is like.

Our challenge, whether we're currently in the cultural majority or the minority, is to find a way to see beyond the labels and seek out our similarities. As an American Latina, I see the common ties that bind us together. This is because I grew up with one foot in each culture: I wouldn't know how to separate them if I tried. It's like *café con leche*—a 50/50 mixture where you don't know where the coffee ends and the milk begins. I don't know where my cultural identities end and begin, but I know I am complete. This is the only way I know how to view myself. My Latino heritage and American heritage are not an either/or proposition: I am Latina, I am American, I am one Cristina with one collective identity that I wear proudly every day. Whether I am speaking Spanish or English, this is my American identity.

As a nation, though, we are having an identity crisis. We don't know who we are anymore. We used to be one cohesive population of many individuals with many different voices, all raised in our love for America. But that cohesiveness, the strength of our patriotism, our love of country is crumbling. We have ripped apart our once "indivisible" nation into confused pieces with no unifying thread. Individual citizens with unique backgrounds, identities, opinions, and knowledge have been slapped with overly simplified labels, creating an "us vs. them" atmosphere of chaos, hurt, and hate. Rather than seeking common ground and values as Americans, we look for and exploit our differences instead.

When we spot those differences in each other, this is when the worst of the human spirit kicks in and we stop listening to each other. Our assumptions and our upbringings replace common sense, and we fire back with weapons of superiority, ego, and hate.

These differences that divide us—which are fueled additionally by politicians, the media, and even each other's comments on social media—are becoming stronger by the day. The United States of America, once known as "The Great Melting Pot," is now "The Great Boiling Pot." Our crisis of national identity is staining the stars and stripes with the blood of a new social civil war. This, however, is unlike our first Civil War. This time, we all live on the battleground, and the shots of hatred, ignorance, and division being fired every day are weakening us as individuals and as a country.

This book is my declaration of resistance: my vow to fight against this overwhelming tide of negativity. It is my attempt to remind us all of the common values and ground that we share: our American identity. I love this country. I am proud to be Red, White, and Latina, which is exactly why I chose that title for this book.

Red, White, and Latina is meant to be unifying, not divisive, as is the case with too many other cultural conversations in America. Many of us seem to be struggling to understand how a person born outside our country can come to love America and be a true patriot. I know that immigrants are some of our most passionate patriots: starting businesses, playing for our revered sports teams, contributing to science and technology, serving in our armed forces, and participating in every part of American culture.

In reality, other than Native Americans, we are all immigrants. When we embrace where we come from and where we are now, we embrace our American identity and become true patriots. We are all red, white, and something, and your "something" doesn't make you any more or less special than anyone else. We're *all* Americans, and it's about time we started acting like it.

1

THE POWER OF MY AMERICAN DREAM

When I am asked about my background, I tell this story: Referring to America as "the land of possibility and potential," my parents moved from Colombia to the Bronx in 1963. My father came to New York to pursue his dream of becoming a surgeon and providing a better life for his family. While pursuing this dream, he withstood unspeakable discrimination, and was confronted with outright hatred, simply because he was an immigrant.

Although he was an educated man, my father did not speak perfect English. As a result, he was seen as a lesser man than those around him. He was judged on his looks and his accent, and was forced to take any type of employment that was offered—from janitor to factory worker—just to support his family. But he never complained. Despite these hard times, my father knew that this incredible country would eventually open its doors to him and his family. He was right. After 30 years of perseverance, hard work, and overcoming many challenges, my father finally accomplished his goal. He became a top surgeon, earning top honors and recognition in the process.

This is the story of one American immigrant, and there are millions more that we all share. I appreciate the opportunities this country has given to my family and to me. Through hard work and dedication, my mother and father made a life for themselves, my sister, my brother, and me. And with my father's help, support, and example, nine of his brothers and sisters eventually emigrated to the US from Colombia. Our lives were full of challenges, but our family always was full of love; I relied on them and their example. My parents' sacrifice allowed us the freedom to excel in the US—and more importantly, it opened doors that have given me access to better opportunities and a better way of life.

I often wonder if the way I tell the story of my father is an overly idealistic view of the American Dream. Is it still true that with a dream, some personal resilience, hard work, and tenacity, anyone can come to this country and make their dreams come true? Or am *I* dreaming? Is the American Dream truly accessible to all equally?

There seems to be a growing divide between the "old" and "new" Americas; my country or yours. We wave the American flag at each other and the middle finger at those we see as outsiders. On one hand, we celebrate a nation originally founded on diversity and a ferociously independent spirit of tolerance. On July 4th we grill burgers and hot dogs, wave flags, and parade in the streets celebrating the idea of that America. But walking the walk throughout the rest of the year is a different story.

The real story of America is written every day, when we accept the challenge to look past labels, see a person's worth, and lay personal judgment aside. It is the story of building bridges to bring out the best, rather than the worst, in each other.

There are those who agree passionately with everything I've just said, but whose actions speak differently than their words. They pay lip service to their love of America, but then do and say things that go blatantly against what America stands for. We like to say we have progressed beyond the labels, last names, skin color, and culture. But we haven't really progressed, have we?

With this level of confusion about what America itself represents, the American Dream might not be as straightforward as my idealized version: "come to this country, work hard, pay your dues, believe, and all your dreams will come true."

As much as it pains me to say it, the perfectionism and exceptionalism represented by the American Dream might be going to our heads a little. These rose-colored (or red, white, and blue-colored) glasses could be blinding us from the reality of our problems. To be blunt: Are we so full of ourselves as Americans that we think others are unworthy of joining us here?

Our struggles with immigration, and the obstacles we're creating around it, are completely against the spirit of inclusion we've always stood for as a country. America is touted as the most welcoming, diverse country in the world—but with the growing *intolerance* of diversity we're seeing in America, we are turning our greatest strength into a weakness.

We used to welcome newcomers to our nation with open arms, with the knowledge that they would bring positive contributions to our workforce. Immigrants once embodied an old-fashioned, hard-working laborers' spirit which became synonymous with the American Dream itself. We took great pride in this work ethic and the ambition to do whatever it took to succeed in this country: it was what we stood for. What happened to our ability to look past labels and see the worth of a human being?

I am not saying we should open the floodgates and allow *anyone* into the US. Rather, I am highlighting that our current disdain for people wishing to become American citizens defies logic. We want to grow and make forward progress as a nation, but we refuse to open our borders to the best and the brightest; we preach diversity, but slam the door in immigrants' faces.

What happened? In the current climate of fear and suspicion surrounding immigrants, are we flatly rejecting their hard-working spirit and will to succeed? It's possible that these individuals understand the true spirit of America *better than many Americans do*. They see that our diverse nation somehow manages to come together, as many different people from all backgrounds, ancestries, ethnicities, and walks of life, to create the foundation of one great country.

How *does* such a diverse mix of people form one United States of America? What is the thing that unites us? Whether your ancestors are recent arrivals, or immigrated further back in history, the answer is the same for each American: we are united by our love of country. We love our country unconditionally, and our country loves us right back. She embraces us across all of our cultures. The Statue of Liberty's script cannot be rewritten;

it is set in stone, and has been for more than a century. She is designed to welcome each and every one of us—every story, every background, and with every passing generation. Lady Liberty has always accepted us each the way we are, and she always will.

On a family trip back to New York City, my husband Christopher and our daughter Sofia and I visited the famous statue. We walked through her museum; saw how she was built, sent over in pieces from France; and the rest of the familiar narrative. Then we arrived at a section of the museum dedicated to a different story: the human one. The three of us read through letter after letter from the people who sacrificed everything to come to our country. After often-harrowing escapes from their homelands and miserable journeys across the ocean, full of pain, sickness, death, and other horrors, Lady Liberty was the first thing they would see rising up from the mist as they neared the end of their journey to freedom. Over and over, their heart-wrenching letters expressed what the sight and the experience meant to them.

On a plaque at the Statue of Liberty museum, you can read letters and diaries penned by some of these immigrants. Here are two that we found most inspiring:

She was a beautiful sight after a miserable crossing. She held such promise for us all with her arm flung high, the torch lighting the way to a new world.

—Unidentified immigrant

You, American born, can never imagine how we, who lived under all kinds of 'isms,' felt when we, in the early hours of a very cold

January morning, saw you, The Statue of Liberty. To us, you meant real freedom. Thank God we made it.
—**Stelio M. Stelson**, from Turkey, 1972

Do Americans today fully understand the promise our young country made to those people, the promise it continues to make generation after generation? I believe my daughter understood when I made the analogy of her grandparents: what they sacrificed and the trauma they endured in their early years here. I could see she was moved. What about her peers, my own peers, and even members of older generations who may not understand (and should know better)? Do we truly understand what the Statue of Liberty meant to those who gave up everything just to see her for the first time?

The Statue of Liberty is supposed to represent acceptance and welcome to all people who share America's ideals of life, liberty, and the pursuit of happiness. It is a visual reminder that with those three things as common denominators for acceptance, any other differences can be resolved. Welcoming us all with open arms, the statue reminds us that our uniqueness and diversity can bring us together, not drive us apart.

Yet here we are, all these years later, being driven apart—by a variety of controversial issues, where our diversity is being used to fuel the fire rather than extinguish it. Conversations about our differences, rather than our similarities, continue to divide us more and more by the day. We can't allow this to happen.

There is too much at stake to risk falling down now. When the country falters, so does the dream it represents. This is dangerous because, as powerful as we are, America is still a young country—especially in comparison to other countries with centuries or millennia of history. What defines our identity and makes us different? What will give us the power to survive, especially in turbulent times like these? What will give us the strength that other superpowers have to stand the test of time?

The answer is simple: our strength lies in the power of the American Dream and one strong, unified American identity. The power of the American Dream is the power we have to welcome many backgrounds and stories, and to blend them together into one American spirit. This will be America's legacy. But each one of us must contribute.

The power of my American Dream is the power of the legacy I will leave for my daughter, and the legacy you will leave for your children. It is a legacy of opportunity; a legacy of faith; a legacy of identity; a legacy of commitment; a legacy of having a voice; and a legacy of believing in yourself, your future, and the futures of your children.

I once asked my father what he felt to be the American Dream, and he replied: "It's simple: the opportunity to work, to raise and provide for my family, and for my children to obtain the best education possible." He added, "What you can do in this country, you cannot do anywhere else in the world."

Now is the time for each of us to ask ourselves: What is the power of *my* American Dream? And how can I use it to help restore our identity as a unified nation—one voice at a time? We are at a national crossroads, one that may ultimately make or break us as a country. Like so many other crises in our history, this too shall pass—but only if we do something about it, together. This unified vision and cohesive voice is what will truly make us a lasting superpower in the world for generations to come.

2

TERRORISM

We maintain the peace through our strength; weakness only invites aggression.

—Ronald Reagan

What is the first thing you think when you see the name of a city appear on your Twitter or Facebook trending list? #Boston, #SanBernardino, #Orlando, #Dallas, #Paris . . . My heart immediately sinks to my stomach, because I know the city name is probably not trending for a good reason. With a racing mind, I click on the hashtag and sure enough, there's often a gruesome news report revealing the loss of life, a dagger stabbed through the hearts of families, and a violent disruption of what was, only hours earlier, a normal day. Terrorism, whether international or domestic, has struck again.

For those of us not connected to anything or anyone involved—the Internet bystanders and looky-loos—this experience is slightly surreal. We know that something awful has happened, and through that awareness, we feel compelled to react.

Since the Internet is the place where most of us are alerted to breaking news, it seems only natural that it's the first place we go to react to it. We go online to make sense of tragic, often complicated events, often before we ever seek out the presence of a single physical human being. Technology is amazing, it is versatile, and it creates incredible convenience in our lives. But should it be the place we go to seek comfort in the face of tragedy? Does technology-based interaction have the psychological depth to grapple with complex human emotions? The Internet wasn't designed for grief counseling; it was not intended as a place to deal with trauma, yet that's exactly how we're using it.

The problem with turning to the Internet in times of tragedy, as opposed to face-to-face interaction, is that when we vent our emotions onto the screen, pouring our hearts out next to the blinking cursor, it can easily lead to miscommunications. Profound levels of sadness, anxiety, anger, and even rage spark heated debates.

When a violent news story changes the whole course of a day, the conversations usually go down a few predictable paths. The names of those paths are: "thoughts and prayers," "ban all guns," and "build the wall, deport the different people, trust no one." Comments like these fill neverending social media threads, and quite often it's obvious that some of the commenters haven't even clicked on or read the actual story. People see the hot-button headline and their fingers fly across the keyboard keys, spewing forth an instant kneejerk reaction.

When a police officer shoots a person of color (even if the officer is also a person of color), the instant conclusion is that racism and police brutality must be involved. A middle-aged Caucasian male shooting up a shopping mall is assumed to have a mental illness, to be a "lone wolf," or to be part of a hate group. I can't help but wonder what would be assumed about someone like me if I were somehow accidentally attached to one of those situations. As a Latina woman, what assumptions would be made? What do *your* gender, age, skin color, political leaning, mental health, and other characteristics say about your motives for doing the things you do?

In no small part due to the events of 9/11, these assumptions have particularly been directed toward individuals who appear to be from the Middle East. Many Americans are struggling to understand the language and labels of Arab vs. Muslim vs. Islam (the former is a culture and ethnicity, the second is a person, the third is a religious ideology). Many other Americans have already made up their minds: if you look Middle Eastern, they assume automatically that your intentions are dangerous and that you shouldn't be in the US. It's only natural to fear evil, especially after one of the biggest tragedies in our country's history, where thousands of innocent lives were lost at the hands of terrorists (who were from the Middle East). But fear has now turned into ignorance, which in turn has fueled demands for walls, deportations, and tougher national border control policies. What began as a national security issue has now morphed into a political wildfire, and beyond that, a cultural phenomenon of demanding a scapegoat on whom to pin our problems, worries, and fears.

This confusion has led to a dangerous habit of grouping together immigrants and terrorists as one and the same. This is once again the lazy, ignorant path of least intellectual resistance. Associating the word "immigrant" with the worst evils in the world is leading us down a dangerous path of not asking the right questions or gathering the right facts. The automatic assumption that anyone who wants to come to America is not to be trusted—that is not what America represents. Naturally, these newcomers could be terrorists, but so could American-born citizens. Immigration doesn't create terrorists. People converting to terrorism creates terrorists.

In addition to the blatant assumptions and stereotyping, the scariest element of these online screamfests is the speed at which they progress. In a few seconds, and based on a single headline, a social media user with strong opinions on issues like the ones above can act as fact-finder, lawyer, judge, jury, and executioner. They can do this without waiting for a single fact about the situation. Then, they can sit and wait for someone to dare disagree—so they have a reason to attack. When the actual facts of the tragedy are revealed and people find their opinions on the wrong side of the truth, it can be very disappointing and even humiliating. Enter the conspiracy theories and "secret truths"—and meanwhile, the social media threads get longer and longer, the fighting becomes more personal and vicious, and nothing is resolved, especially for those who lost their lives and the loved ones left behind. Within days or weeks, the incident is forgotten . . . until another ominous city name with a hashtag shows up, and we rinse and repeat.

What are we accomplishing here? Are we launching into virtual civil battles so quickly that we're completely trampling any hope of ever coming together as a country and making progress on an issue?

When it comes to terrorism, it seems as if we are *terrorizing* as much as we're *being terrorized*. Are our differences of opinion preventing us from hearing each other?

COURT OF PUBLIC OPINION

Is it possible to believe passionately about one side of an issue, without being willing to at least listen to the other side? I've had the opportunity to study this phenomenon as a television court judge for over a decade.

Overseeing small claims cases, it is my job to look at both sides of the story. The beauty of court television is that it allows both sides to present their point of view with more emotion, and in greater detail, than they would in a "normal" small claims courtroom. The arguments I hear are passionate, often fiery, and always reveal where each person is coming from on a personal level. Ruling on these cases has taught me how to listen to and understand both sides of an argument while managing erupting emotions, which can be the most difficult part. In addition to hearing the facts and reviewing the evidence, I also hear the frustration, the contempt, the hurt, the betrayal and all the other human emotions that bring people into my courtroom when they cannot agree on a resolution to a problem. There are no arguments for the sake of arguments. Every dispute has two sides to the story.

When it comes to terrorism, the two arguments seem to be either for going to extremes and doing whatever it takes to make ourselves safe, or denying that there's a threat at all and going about our lives in blissful ignorance. To some, this is the difference between total safety and total liberty. But are either of these extremes actually the best solution for keeping us safe?

Total Safety

On one side of the terrorism argument, we have those who see the threats to our safety—as individuals and as a nation. They recognize the volatile, unpredictable world we live in, are legitimately concerned for their own safety and secure future, and that of their family, friends, and neighbors. As a result, many believe in the need for full gun rights (including open carry in public areas), secure borders, and restrictive immigration laws. As self-proclaimed historical purists, they point to the United States Constitution, particularly the Second Amendment, which protects our right to bear arms.

These people see legal, concealed carry weapon holders as adjuncts to law enforcement: they carry a gun not to harm their neighbor, but to protect him or her. They also see evidence of terrorism threats on the rise in countries with strict gun laws and open borders, where free citizens are "sitting ducks" for the bad guys. They argue that our founding fathers, by all accounts, wanted American citizens to be able to protect themselves from each other, from foreign threats, and from tyranny within their own government. They also point out that a secure, safe country is a more stable, prosperous one, thinking of the futures of our children and grandchildren.

The "total safety" believers tend to give law enforcement officers and members of the armed forces the benefit of the doubt, since they believe that the majority of them are good people, committed to protecting the public. When they do hear about a cop shooting, there's a piece of them that believes the "victim" must have done something wrong, or in some way failed to comply with the officer—who was just doing his or her job.

For these points of view, this group is labeled in the court of public opinion as conservative and extreme right wing.

Total Liberty

On the other side of the security issue are those who pride themselves in having more progressive viewpoints of what constitutes a safe and secure nation. They believe that terrorists can exist equally at home and abroad; that an equal, if not greater, threat to American citizens than foreign terrorists comes potentially from members of their own communities. These people see irresponsible, lax gun laws with dangerous loopholes that allow nearly anyone to obtain a deadly firearm with little or no background checking or training.

This group sees their country becoming increasingly armed and potentially unpredictable, and this scares them—especially those with children. Like those favoring "total safety," these individuals are also concerned with leaving a secure, safe, stable and prosperous country for their children and grandchildren.

As much as they hear from the other side that most gun owners are law abiding, trained, mentally stable citizens, the news stories about mass shootings, gun "accidents," and guns getting into the hands of mentally ill people and criminals are proof that the laws are not working. The best solution, in this group's opinion, is to restrict access to certain types of guns and to require better background checks, in hopes of closing the loopholes that allow these mistakes to happen.

When it comes to our borders, believers in total liberty can't understand how those on the other side see immigrants and refugees as "threats" when they believe that anyone, from anywhere can be equally threatening or non-threatening—that it is our responsibility as the world's leading humanitarian democracy to welcome all immigrants into America with open arms.

Many in this group have recently become distrustful and even afraid of police officers because, honestly, they just don't know what to think anymore. They want to trust law enforcement as protectors of the peace, but with all these instances of apparently innocent African Americans being shot by cops for no good reason—what are we supposed to think?

For these points of view, they are referred to as "bleeding heart liberals" and sometimes even "socialist" or "commies" by the other side.

I would be surprised if at least some of you weren't offended by the way I described these two groups of people and their ideologies. This is –ism thinking. It is deeply rooted in ideology rather than in common sense, a willingness to explore the facts, and the application of deductive reasoning. It might even seem ridiculous reading both wildly extreme points of view here. But this is exactly what SO many of us are doing every day in our conversations. We are making massive, usually fear-based assumptions about other people's beliefs and values and jumping to conclusions, never bothering to ask people on both sides what they really think and why they think it, or to research the facts.

CLOSING ARGUMENT

What happens when the two sides collide, and we must find the balance of safety and liberty in a horrifying real-life scenario? We all remember the 2013 Boston Marathon bombing. But how many of us remember some of the events that came after the bombing, when one of the terrorist brothers lay dead and the other, Dzhokhar Tsarnaev, was placed on trial for his crimes? There was one event in particular that got my blood boiling and raised some questions for me, like: Do we even recognize terrorism when we see it? In our efforts to be fair and deliver justice for all, do we sometimes go too far, treating the bad guys much better than they deserve? Where is the boundary between liberty and the perception of being pushovers?

Did you know that after the marathon bombings, the family of Dzhokhar Tsarnaev was allowed to enter America—on our dime—for the sentencing phase of his trial? They arrived to convince the judge not to hand down the death penalty as a sentence (though he ultimately did, with an appeal currently being planned by Tsarnaev's attorneys at the time of this writing). Not only that, but they were put up at a fairly nice hotel outside of Boston, again on our dime. The Tsarnaev family members were later moved out of the hotel, after hotel guests started checking out and presumably angry locals began gathering outside. Our federal government added that emergency relocation and new housing to the tab, along with around the clock 24/7 security by three agencies: the FBI, US Marshals, and the local police. The total estimated taxpayer bill to accommodate this family of terrorists totaled over $100,000. Meanwhile, those injured in the attack and the families of those killed could not even get their parking reimbursed to attend the trial.

Remember that Tsarnaev and his brother (who was killed in a shootout with police following the bombing, taking one police officer's life with him) are terrorists. They created military grade explosives, similar to the kinds of IEDs you'd find in the Middle East, that blew the legs off marathon runners and bystanders. The bombs the two brothers made killed the victims, including a young child, by tearing through their organs—leaving the victims to bleed to death on the sidewalks near the marathon finish line.

Tsarnaev's family members arrived in America to declare that it was Dzhokhar's domineering brother's fault. They claimed Dzhokhar was just the innocent younger brother, being bullied into going along with the plan. I don't buy it. A killer is a killer; a terrorist is a terrorist. If you're a good person, can you get talked into murdering innocent people? Let's also not forget the jail-cell footage that jurors saw during the trial, of Tsarnaev giving the middle finger to the security camera in his cell—giving America the finger.

And the family of the bombers? Here's what Tsarnaev's mother said after her son was found guilty: "They [the US] will pay for my sons and the sons of Islam, permanently!"

Emotions aside, I understand why our country did this for the Tsarnaev family. Dzhokhar was a citizen of the United States, and our Constitution protected him. But I was still frustrated at the morally lenient way that we all approached the situation. I wondered, were we so focused on being fair that we were being pushovers? Did we recognize people who would do such horrible things to innocent Americans as the enemy?

As Americans, do we truly understand the definition of the word enemy today? Especially in contrast to times like the World Wars, where enemies came from specific countries with clearly defined borders? In the past, we were at war with *countries*, not groups of people scattered geographically around the whole world. Therefore, we assumed we knew how to spot them and label them as our enemies.

But the fact is, enemies are people who will kill you anytime and anywhere. They are people who want us dead only because we are Americans. And whether we're in denial or not, they exist. If you don't believe me, ask the people of France, Syria, and other countries where missions of hate have led to the massacres of innocent people. Are we still back under the post-9/11 perception that the terrorists just don't understand us—that maybe if they got to know America and how great we are, we could make them like us? You can't make your enemies like you. Unfortunately, reality just doesn't work that way.

What I didn't understand, at the time, was how our perceptions of the bad guy went from misinformed to downright delusional. Just a few months after the Boston marathon bombing, *Rolling Stone* magazine put Tsarnaev—the now convicted terrorist—on the cover of its magazine. Many people, especially in New England, were outraged and appalled at the lack of common sense displayed by *Rolling Stone* and the media in general. Did the media's lack of common sense then seep into our federal government, resulting in the family of a terrorist being treated *better* than the family of the victims? Remember, this family simultaneously declared Dzhokhar's innocence and America's guilt.

What happens to a country that forgets how to identify its own enemies and therefore protect itself against them? Even animals in nature recognize their enemies and take actions to ensure their survival. By leaning too far in the direction of liberty, without regard for our own security, are we putting ourselves at risk for extinction? Where is the balance?

VERDICT

In the case of total safety vs. total liberty, my ruling is this: Personal liberty and common sense must go hand in hand. Common sense and a sense of caution must guide our personal liberties.

We all have our own beliefs about the proper balance of liberty and government oversight: how much government is "enough," which laws are fair and which are unfair, and how to make the world a safer place. Those who run for public office have the opportunity to act on those beliefs. The rest of us have the opportunity to make our voices heard through voting (and not just every four years, either). Lawyers and judges interpret and uphold the laws. For every one of us, it is our responsibility to educate ourselves on *both* sides of every issue, listen to all opinions, and do our best to persuade the lawmakers to represent us fairly.

In our daily lives, it's also worth recognizing that we are closer to the middle ground than we think. When it comes to the issues discussed in this chapter, whether you consider yourself conservative, liberal, or somewhere in between, I'm willing to go out on a limb and guess that you share the same core beliefs and concerns as your counterparts. As an American you likely possess an innate sense of justice and fairness. You want to see people who commit crimes be brought to justice. But you also want to protect those who have committed *no* crimes and are unfairly targeted because of the color of their skin. Especially in the wake of acts of terrorism or other tragedies, you're troubled when innocent people are punished by association.

Nevertheless, during these times of tension, you're concerned for your own safety and that of your family. With each new, horrifying headline, you wonder if this will get worse before it gets better.

As citizens, we have no control over when, where, or how an act of terrorism will unfold—at a sporting event, in a nightclub, on an army base, or otherwise. In most cases we will never truly understand the motives of the terrorist(s), as much as we speculate. What we do have control over is the way in which we respond.

When you see the city name with the hashtag in front of it, you may have an immediate emotional response. Something inside you screams "Stop! No more." I'm with you, especially as a mother, responsible for another life and constantly concerned about the world in which my daughter is growing up.

It is how you decide to act on that emotion—how we all decide—that can be a closed door or a turning point. After your initial moment of horror, after the thoughts and prayers, what will you choose to do from there? Will you take to social media and pick fights with those who disagree with you, attempting to bully them into submission? Or will you look for the opportunity to learn something new about the subject that you didn't know before? Or, will you follow the easiest intellectual route and pick an extreme to align yourself with?

Recall the arguments earlier in this chapter for "total safety" and "total liberty." One of the reasons for those arguments was to make the point of how ridiculous and illogical it is to be "100%" anything, whether extreme left or extreme right. In a country as diverse as America, extreme thinking is nothing but a recipe for division and disaster, as people from each end of the spectrum try to bend others to their will. This is ironic when it comes to the subject of terrorism, since terrorism itself typically comes from its own extremist ideology. Do we honestly believe that we can fix it with our own extreme thinking?

3

THE "A WORD"

I can't claim to know the words of all the national anthems in the world, but I don't know of any other that ends with a question and a challenge as ours does: Does that flag still wave o'er the land of the free and the home of the brave? That is what we must all ask.

—Ronald Reagan

No, the "A word" is not the word you're thinking of, the one you might use when you get cut off in traffic. Believe it or not, the "A word" I mean is "America." Apparently the word "America" is now considered offensive. Even beyond the word itself, symbols representing America, like our flag and national anthem, seem to be included in a new unspoken category of national offense.

Let me offer some evidence, by way of our younger generation. At first glance, these might seem like fairly harmless examples of young people engaging in activities that aren't very serious. It might even be easy to chalk these stories up as nothing more than over-dramatized, media sensationalism. What if, however, we looked at these same stories from the standpoint that today's young people are tomorrow's torchbearers of our American identity? From that angle, these stories about kids making harmless choices might actually be seeds of future unity problems.

In March of 2015, a student at the University of California at Irvine submitted a resolution to ban the American flag from lobby areas of student government offices on campus. One of the twenty-five reasons the student listed for his proposed ban was that the American flag could symbolize "exceptionalism and superiority" to some. The ban was narrowly approved by student legislators in a 6-4 vote, but later vetoed by the school's executive council.

When I first read this, I couldn't help but wonder how many of the students in favor of the resolution are attending UC Irvine courtesy of scholarships or student loans funded by the exact government and taxpayers they're accusing of promoting exceptionalism and superiority. Also, when did aiming to be exceptional become a bad thing? As a country, we are developing a bad habit of getting so wrapped up in the activism that we don't think through all the details of issues. More on that later, but let's move onto the next example of citizens evidently being embarrassed by their own country.

At a high school in New Mexico, the student event planning committee chose communism as the theme of their upcoming prom. Communism. On top of that, the students seemed genuinely surprised when their decision caused a stir within the community. If these kids didn't understand why choosing communism as a theme for their prom was upsetting to people, wouldn't that make our educational institutions a complete failure when it comes to teaching world history?

If these students failed to understand that a bloody, violent and oppressive chapter of world history was not an appropriate party theme, then we have failed to teach the next generation how to avoid the mistakes of our collective past. Ask any person who has suffered the consequences of communism, including people from communist nations who sacrificed everything to escape to America, and they will tell you that communism is no cause for celebration. The question to ask ourselves is: Did the students make this choice out of pure ignorance, or was it a result of being embarrassed by their own national culture and political ideology (which of course is in exact opposition to communism)? Was it their way of rebelling against what America stands for?

Here's another example of a student event planning gone awry. Lexington, Massachusetts is the town where the first shot of the American Revolutionary War was fired, called "the shot heard 'round the world." A couple of years ago at Lexington High School the theme of a dance was changed from "American Pride" to "National Pride." School officials went on record saying they: "wanted the dance to be more inclusive so students could represent their different nationalities." Wasn't the idea behind the original theme to celebrate America's independence and those who fought for it? Are we trying to become so inclusive that we risk excluding our own national history? Why can't we all be American *and* still take pride in our cultural identities? We've become completely confused by this extremely limited "either/or" mentality.

It's as if we've decided that in order to be inclusive toward people of other cultures, we need to completely exclude America from the conversation; that we need to turn our backs on our flag, and our history and everything that America stands for.

Let's make up our minds—do we love immigrants or are we threatened by them? They don't appear to be threatened by us, and they certainly aren't offended by America. Newcomers to our country are some of the most patriotic, America-loving people I've met. They understand that America gives them the privilege to maintain and cherish their culture, while pledging allegiance to this country first.

At Lexington High School, a group of students stepped forward and spoke out against the decision to turn "American Pride" into "National Pride." One student was quoted in a local newspaper as saying that he "felt the decision was ridiculous and based on hypersensitivity to being politically correct."

Another student said, "People consider America to be a melting pot, so the fact that it was even considered offensive is what people are a little surprised about."

What a smart observation. Yes—what happened to that sense of unity and open-mindedness? Have we lost our way as a nation that stands solid in its history and values? Do we feel that, in order to be a good host to other cultures, we need to completely abandon our nationality as Americans?

In these examples (and too many others like them) our citizens appear to be embarrassed by and apologetic for the symbols, history, culture, and ideology associated with America. It's not okay that we're condoning this message in younger generations. It's not okay to be embarrassed by your own country. Because if it is, we're setting a dangerous precedent.

I wonder if we've raised the bar too high and we're looking for something perfect to be proud of. I understand that our country is not perfect. Our history is not spotless. Ignorance, violence, and war still exist. But I would challenge you to show me a country that *is* perfect. Show me a nation with a spotless record. I doubt you'll find one, because countries are nothing but a collection of people, flawed works-in-progress called human beings. Is the collection of people called "America" so bad, so flawed, and so destructive, that we need to be embarrassed by our own country? Are we so awful that we need to hide our flag in shame, pretend our history never happened, and turn a blind eye to all the great things about America?

So many men and women have died, and are continuing to die, for our country. This is like saying to them: "Thanks but no thanks; you didn't have to do that. This country isn't worth fighting and dying for." That would be a tragic message to send and represent. I see more good than bad in our country and in the American people. Of course I see things that need to be improved upon and changed for the better, but there is a big difference between change and outright embarrassment for who we are, inherently, as a nation.

Beyond being embarrassed, it seems that some people even find it "cool" to find America offensive. They believe that rejecting everything America stands for creates the appearance of being a progressive deep thinker and conscientious objector. Intelligence and patriotism do not have to live on separate islands. As a matter of fact, when we dig deeper and look at the idea that mocking America somehow makes you a more progressive thinker, there is a major flaw in that argument: When we reject America to make a point, we reject the very freedom that *allows* us to make that point in the first place.

There is a famous professional quarterback who protested the national anthem at his football games, to make a point. After creating media shockwaves by sitting on the team bench during the national anthem at a pre-season game, San Francisco 49ers quarterback Colin Kaepernick said this in the post-game press conference when asked if he would continue to sit: "I'll continue to sit. I'm going to stand with the people that are being oppressed. To me this is something that has to change and when there's significant change and I feel like that flag represents what it's supposed to represent in this country—is representing the way that it's supposed to—I'll stand."

I managed to create mini-shockwaves of my own after releasing my response on social media to Kaepernick's choice. Here is what I posted.

Thank you dummy, for reminding us that that the flag symbolizes our deep rooted belief that everyone has the undeniable right to be free in every way, and to express that. While I will not condone what he did, because it is repulsive, I will thank him for making me realize that the red white and blue deserves to be flown with dignity, respect, and pride. I'm going to go have my husband put our flag out now—why wait for July 4th anymore? I will also take this opportunity to thank all of those who fight for HIS right to be an idiot. THEY are the true heroes!

Because of that flag, because of that national anthem he was protesting, Kaepernick had the right to sit, and I had the right to respond, uncensored, with my opinion of his actions.

There were many who agreed with my opinion, as well as those who accused me of being unfair and criticizing me for resorting to name-calling. I will now admit, in retrospect, that I regret using the words "dummy" and "idiot" in the heat of the moment. To be blunt, I saw that guy sitting on the bench during the playing of my national anthem, and I got angry. I thought of all the soldiers who fought and died, and are continuing to fight and die for our flag . . . and I got emotional. I took to the Internet where my fingers outran my better judgment. For that, I apologize.

Ultimately, this incident was a powerful reminder of one of the same lessons I've learned and am now writing about in this book. It reminded me to stop, take a breath, and look at both sides of a story first without immediately rushing to judgment or jumping to conclusions.

The fact is that America allows each one of us to have and share our opinion, whether it's well thought-out or fired off in the heat of the moment. But the more interesting and important conversation that emerged was about Kaepernick's patriotism, and how patriotic it was to criticize him. Some took it so far as to say that criticizing his choice to sit was unpatriotic. Is it really a sign of patriotism to say that anyone is immune from criticism? Especially when they are protesting one of the greatest symbols of our patriotism, the flag and national anthem. When it comes to the relationship between protesting and patriotism, I fear we might have it backwards.

Without the umbrella of America and all her tenets of freedom and liberty, what is the source of our protests? Just like parents can love their children but disagree with their actions, we can still love our country while disagreeing with some of its actions. But if you blatantly disagree with and turn your back on your country, you are no longer protesting an issue; you are now protesting the thing that allows you to even speak up in the first place. "America" comes first, and your frustration with the system comes second. If you disrespect the first, you will never have the freedom to speak out against the second.

I believe this is where well-intentioned protesters like Kaepernick are getting confused. I admire him for trying to make a point and use his high-profile voice to speak up for those who cannot do so for themselves (or, certainly, as loudly). But isn't the way he chose to act on that intention ultimately hurting America and everything we stand for? Shouldn't he be protesting the police instead of the flag? The majority of the attention Kaepernick received in the weeks following was for the disrespect he had shown for his country, rather than for any increased awareness around the issue of police brutality or racial oppression. Whether you are White, Black, Hispanic, Asian, Middle Eastern or otherwise; whether you were born here or immigrated to America; I believe you should always respect your flag. Period. If Kaepernick continues to disrespect the most valuable symbol of who we all are—the visual representation of our collective American identity—the spotlight will continue to shine on *him*, rather than on the issue he wants to bring to our attention. Is this the most effective way to move forward the conversation about how to stop oppressing minorities?

His supporters state that it is. They will tell me I'm absolutely wrong about this. They are also insisting (at fever pitch) that Kaepernick had every right to sit down during the national anthem. I could not agree more! He has every right to express himself freely, just as we all do. We have been afforded this right by the Constitution. However, while the Constitution can safeguard our personal liberties and protect us from tyranny, it can't protect us from our own decisions. Those battling it out as to whether or not he has the right to sit are having the wrong argument. The question may not be "Did he have the right?" but rather "Was it the right decision?"

We all have the right to free speech, but when it comes to the court of common sense we also have the responsibility to think about the consequences of our actions. Just because you have the *right* to do something, should you automatically do it?

COURT OF PUBLIC OPINION

Disrespecting America

There is a group of people that believes that, while the First Amendment gives us the right to say what we want without legal consequences, we're forgetting the real-world consequences of our statements. They believe that when we speak against America, we speak against all who have sacrificed for her flag. These people would remind us all that harsh words can create the image of a country full of people who are ashamed to be here. They point out how these protests against the flag, national anthem, and other symbols of America give the impression of a divided, and therefore weakened, nation.

These people remind us of the expression: "United we stand, divided we fall," and say that when we turn our backs on the flag, we essentially do the same to those who have suffered and died for it. They demand that we remember the importance of taking pride in one's country. They worry that without pride, the future of their country and future generations of citizens, especially their children and grandchildren, is in jeopardy. When they see someone ashamed of America they take it personally.

Free Speech Shows Respect

On the other side is the group who believes that speaking up, protesting, and making our voices heard is what America is all about, and is precisely how change happens. This group says that calmness and complacency bring about no change. They challenge people who call them unpatriotic, with the belief that the most patriotic thing one can do is exercise their free speech as a core American right. They wonder what happened to progress, and question if we're supposed to stay stuck in the past, blindly pledging allegiance to an America that, quite frankly, no longer exists.

CLOSING STATEMENT

There have been times in our history when there was no question of America's greatness. One of those times was in 1961, when President Kennedy declared "We choose the moon!" and announced the formation of NASA to support this goal. At the time of that speech, some people thought JFK was crazy. Going to the moon was something out of a science fiction novel. But eight years later, we did it. It was such a thrilling, proud moment for our nation. In that incredible moment, as we collectively watched our astronauts walk on the moon and plant the American flag on its surface, the "A word" embarrassed nobody; we were all proud Americans.

America, during the time of the space program, represented taking risks, challenging ourselves, and having the courage to do things not because they were easy—but *because they were hard*. Our space program was about science; progress; hope; dreaming; raising the bar higher; and leading the way for the rest of the world. It was one of the greatest accomplishments in our history and one that, as a nation, we were most proud of.

What can we do to get America to dream big like that again? What will it ultimately take to once again rally around our flag, our national anthem, and everything else that represents us?

We rallied together after 9/11 in a powerful, inspiring, and emotional way. We've done so on smaller scales for other tragedies. But those instances should not—and cannot—be the only type of events that unify us. It's the things bigger than ourselves, the times when we come together and shoot for the stars, that remind us of why America is great.

Rather than uniting only in times of tragedy, chaos, and discord, maybe the answer to building pride around the "A word" is another powerful and positive accomplishment like walking on the moon was. When a nation's government puts a stake in the ground, like JFK did with that mission to go to the moon, it creates an immediate, electrifying national excitement. It rallies the entire country around an empowering, unyielding will to succeed. Because when our country wins, so do its people.

Maybe that's what those high school and college students in the stories, along with the football quarterback, were really trying to communicate through their actions: "Give me something bigger and better to believe in. I want to love America, but I need some help finding a good reason."

Unfortunately, though, loving your country is an unconditional deal—not unlike marriage and family. Whether you realize it or not, you pledged your allegiance to America at birth, when you arrived, or when your ancestors before you did. Just because she's not always perfect, doesn't mean you have the right to turn your back on America and everything she stands for. She's not asking you to pledge your allegiance blindly, but she does ask that you do it loyally. Isn't that the least we all can do?

VERDICT

My verdict on the "A word," and differentiating between patriotic protest versus potentially damaging protest, is this: Look at the big picture. Look at the overall pattern of behavior in the person protesting. Protest for the right reason.

Because it comes down to character and the person's intentions. Are they acting on behalf of themselves, or on behalf of the cause itself? Is this a selfish or selfless protest? Do they want what's best for their country—or for themselves?

The most successful, notable activists throughout history had patterns of selfless behavior and commitment to their cause. Their long-term reputations were built on more than their actions and media soundbites. The individuals who successfully created change in America ultimately put their country before themselves. Rather than leading from a place of embarrassment and shame, they led from a love of country so powerful that they wanted to make it better.

When you make the choice to be embarrassed by the "A word," you are not leading from a place of love and pride in your country. If you don't love the freedoms reflected in the American flag, how can you expect to reap the benefits of those freedoms?

4

GET IN LINE

This country was built on immigrants. People who were brave enough to start over. How strong we are to leave behind everything we know in hopes of something better. We are not fearless, we just have dreams bigger than our fears.
— **Camila Cabello** (Fifth Harmony)

ARE YOU HUNGRY?

I t may seem inappropriate that I'm quoting a teenager on such a serious subject as immigration. But we all know that young people, in their innocence, sometimes possess a wisdom beyond their years.

The quote above is from one of the singers in my daughter's favorite band—who happens to be an immigrant. Sofia brought me to tears when she showed me an essay that Camila Cabello, a member of Fifth Harmony, wrote about her family's story of coming to America.

Born in Havana, Cuba to a Cuban mother and Mexican father, Camila was shuttled back and forth between Havana and Mexico City before her family finally made the decision to immigrate to the United States. The decision forced her mother to give up her career as an architect. For her father, it was worse: he would later risk his life to cross the Mexico-US border and reunite with his family. While these are familiar chapters of the American story, it was something else Camila wrote about so eloquently that tugged at my heart: the hunger. "Immigrants have one thing in common: hunger. I don't mean it literally, although that's true too, but metaphorically. The hunger to do the impossible because you have no choice, because you came too damn far, because you've known what struggling is, and you're not going to take an opportunity for granted."

For me, this hits the absolute heart of what drives the immigrant spirit: to fight, to persist, and ultimately to succeed. Immigrants are driven by a hunger for a better life, a hunger to work hard, a hunger to do the impossible, and a hunger to be Americans. While many of us hope and pray for a better life for ourselves, how many of us risk it all to ensure a better life for our children?

Future generations will be tasked with carrying the torch—for this "better life" and for what defines us as Americans—into a chapter of history that has yet to unfold. They shouldn't be driven to dismiss this hunger and spirit as a result of misguided fear and suspicion directed toward immigrants. This would be cheating younger generations from learning valuable lessons about struggle, hard work, and opportunity—lessons that are an integral part of our history.

Instead of talking about building walls, we should be sharing stories about moving mountains. Those who fear immigrants need to hear the stories of these individuals, driven by an insatiable hunger that makes them willing to risk everything to be in America. I've always believed that in difficult times, it's the often-forgotten human story that helps us decipher the real dilemma. Once we understand the human story, it changes our perspective and makes us more empathetic. Without the human story, however, we lose this rational perspective and often allow irrational fears to overpower our thinking.

Our fears around immigrants, in large part, are the result of a messy, widespread set of misconceptions about the people who come to America (and how they do it). There is a sizable gap between the perceived problem and the actual situation. The perception is overly simplified, with people demanding that immigrants "get in line." Whenever I hear that, I wonder if they think of our borders as being akin to a theme park—take a number, wait your turn, and file into America in an orderly fashion. Like most pressing national problems, the reality is much more complex.

There are many myths that seem to take hold and replace the truth of America's multi-layered immigration laws. It's easier to believe simplified talking points than it is to make an effort to understand what people actually have to go through in order to immigrate to the United States. But as imperfect our system is, it has stood the test of time—from granting opportunity and freedom to those earliest arrivals on Ellis Island, to serving those today who seek refuge. One thing that immigrants all have in common, then and now, families and individuals, entrepreneurs and professional athletes, is the hunger to succeed.

COURT OF PUBLIC OPINION: FICTION VS. FACTS

When it comes to the facts vs. fiction, how do we know what to believe? For many people, the answer is to believe the thing that's being shouted the loudest and most often. Whether or not this "fact" is actually true is secondary. The bully pulpit is powered by passion, repetition, and strong personal beliefs, but not necessarily facts.

Some of these pieces of fiction are profoundly affecting the actual human lives of immigrants and their families. Fiction is spread when people click a button to share something that *sounds* right before taking the time to determine whether or not it *is* right. But with each click on an untrue talking point, damage is done. Falsehoods are being spread: a plague of ignorance has struck the American masses. For me personally, talking points like the ones that follow are the most sensationalistic: they're oversimplified, easy to latch onto, and easy to parrot and pass along before taking the time to figure out if they're even true. This is also makes talking points like these ones the most dangerous.

#1: They're all criminals and have nothing positive to contribute.

This is a grossly misleading hook that plays into our fear of the unknown and distrust of anyone "not like us." When we're told to be afraid and distrustful, it's much easier to focus on the negative contributions of a group of people, while ignoring the positive contributions.

Not "all immigrants are criminals." Statistically, there are people who commit crimes in *all* communities. Therefore, naturally, yes, there are people who commit crimes and happen to be from other countries. Absolutely untrue, however, is the myth that with more people flowing into the United States, crime rates go up. In fact, statistics show that the arrival of more people into our country actually *decreases* crime rates. Between 1990 and 2013, overall immigration grew from 7.9 percent of the population to 13.1 percent, and 3.5 million undocumented citizens swelled to 11.2 million. In that same time period, FBI crime data revealed that violent crime dropped by 48 percent and property crime by 41 percent. Overall, in 2010 only 1.6 percent of immigrant men between the ages of 18 and 39 were in jail, in contrast to 3.3 percent of American-born men in the same age range.[1]

Some would respond to this by saying that immigrants who commit crimes are somehow slipping through the cracks of the law simply because they are undocumented. This is a myth, and unfortunately a popular one. Undocumented individuals are processed just like anyone else in the criminal justice system. If they commit a crime, they suffer the same consequences as an American-born citizen—while also putting their future legal status into jeopardy. As a matter of fact, we have really tough definitions and standards of criminality that don't apply to US citizens, but *do* apply to immigrants.

If we're actively seeking out reasons to exclude people from society through this kind of stereotyping, and automatically categorizing them as criminals, it prevents us from seeing their

---

1   "Giving the facts a fighting chance"; American Immigration Council, Special Report 2015.

positive contributions. This idea that immigrants are criminals, to be considered a threat to our country until they prove otherwise, is akin to "guilty until proven innocent." It assumes the worst rather than the best about these people, and ignores immigrants' consistent and positive contributions to America. We cannot have a complete conversation without looking at all the individuals who make up this segment of our population—including the ones who come here wishing to contribute their talents to this country, and ultimately succeed.

As of 2010, 18% of all Fortune 500 companies were founded by immigrants, with those companies creating $1.7 trillion in annual revenue and employing 3.6 million employees.[2] In fact, immigrants are almost twice as likely to start businesses than American-born citizens are. In contrast to the myth that immigrants are "taking our jobs," they are actually creators of 10 million American jobs and generators of over $4.2 trillion in revenue.[3] Many of those jobs are in tech: 25% of technology-related companies founded between 1995 and 2005 had founders born outside of the US. Studies show that citizens from other countries who graduate from our universities with advanced degrees in STEM fields each generate, on average, 2.62 jobs for American workers.[4]

Especially in light of the frequently-broadcasted need for better STEM advancements in America to help us remain competitive in

2   "Giving the facts a fighting chance"; American Immigration Council, Special Report 2015.

3   Politifact.com. "Steve Case says 40 percent of the Fortune 500 were started either by immigrants or children of immigrants." July 6, 2011. http://www.politifact.com/truth-o-meter/statements/2011/jul/06/steve-case/steve-case-says-40-percent-fortune-500-were-starte/

4   "Giving the facts a fighting chance"; American Immigration Council, Special Report 2015.

the world, why don't we hear more about positive contributions like these? One reason is that the media spotlight typically falls on criminals more than on innovators, business owners, computer scientists, and engineers (not to mention actors, athletes, and entertainers) who contribute positively to our country. These are the immigrants we should be actively trying to attract and shine a spotlight on: the ones who come here with positive, productive intentions; the ones who reflect our best values as a country. It's our responsibility, then, to dig deeper, see the whole picture, and not just take small slices of it and blow them out of proportion.

Concentrating on a small group of criminals, and ignoring the positive contributions of the rest, adds a disturbing layer of hypocrisy to the debate as a whole. If our goal is to have an honest discussion, let's bring the entrepreneurs, entertainers, athletes, scientists, and job creators to the table. Without their side of the conversation, there is no debate; there is just a set of convenient myths used to propagate fear and hatred toward a group of people.

If, after reading this, you hear the word "immigrant" and you still picture a stereotypical criminal, like in a Hollywood movie; a drug dealer crawling over a wall into America; then you're paying attention only to the negative, while ignoring the positive.

#2: They're trying to cut in line.

Another common piece of oversimplified fiction is that most individuals applying for citizenship want to cheat and circumvent the proper procedures. This idea is especially easy to spread in a country that often seems to live and breathe sports and competition. The idea of "cheating" is relatable, and is also easy to translate into propaganda (especially a 140-character tweet or political talking point). As a culture, we are good at judging what is "fair" and what is not.

This idea of people acting "unfairly" by trying to circumvent the proper paths to citizenship instantly creates fear and anger. Like any other piece of propaganda, the more times people repeat it, the more people believe it—assuming that if this many people are saying it, the claim must be true. Well, I hate to pop any bubbles of self-righteousness (because *your* ancestors clearly played by the rules) but the oversimplified image of this magical line that most immigrants are trying to cut to the front of is outright false.

What many well-meaning people don't understand is that our immigration laws are complicated and constantly changing. There is no way for an individual to simply go and "apply" for a green card. It's not like driving down to your local bank and opening a new account or applying for a passport. Perhaps a big reason behind this "get in line" myth is exactly this—our ease of access to basically anything we want in this country. Based on this, we assume that it's just as easy for others to get on the path to citizenship. Not only is this completely untrue, but the consequences of being unable to easily obtain a green card can be devastating, particularly for families attempting to immigrate here.

The process is completely different now than even when my own parents emigrated from Colombia in the 1960s. In fact, what many of today's proud American citizens don't realize is that, based on our current laws, their own ancestors might not have qualified for legal status.

What about today's scenario though? Are the allegations of cheating or "cutting" true? The reality is, *there is no line* for undocumented individuals who either arrive in America illegally or overstay their legally-obtained visas. In fact, *there is a long list of people* who have gone through the process of legally petitioning for their family to join them in the United States—as well as professionals who, through employment, have legally applied for a green card—and all these people are forced to wait for years because our current laws are out of date. People who properly apply for legal status through employment, family, even refugee or asylum options are faced with obstacles such as eligibility barriers and visa limits by nationality. This is *after* they wait "in line." The available options for people to come here legally are dramatically meager, especially in comparison to today's demand. For this reason and more, the current pathways to United States citizenship are like crumbling old bridges, unable to hold the weight of those trying to cross.

The reality is that even when immigrants do all that we ask of them, they still end up stuck in a ridiculously long wait: a molasses-like slowing of time that seems to serve as punishment rather than reward for obeying the law. How is this fair? The fact is, our current process is extremely *unfair* and creates insurmountable obstacles against those people who do follow the law.

Our overwhelmed, convoluted legal setup is actually splitting up families: some family members are allowed in and others are forced to stay behind, waiting for permission to be reunited with their loved ones. In a country that prides itself on "family values" and promotes the divinity of the traditional family unit, isn't this hypocritical? I find it ironic that some of the same politicians and leaders who preach about family values are the same ones advocating tougher immigration laws—which usually means tossing even more obstacles and barriers into the pathways to citizenship. Even as well-intentioned immigrants follow our laws the best they can, there are a slew of barriers keeping them separated from their loved ones. Therefore, many see no other option than to come here anyway.

For those people—the approximately 11 million undocumented ones who either crossed the border illegally or overstayed their visas— the situation then becomes more complicated than simply to "go back where you came from." It would take decades and billions of dollars to accomplish such a plan, and even if we did, there would be no legal way for them to return to the United States. Is the solution to our flawed legal procedures really to punish those looking for a better life for their children?

On top of that, these are people who have in many cases lived here for years, raising and educating their children; frequently serving in our armed forces; paying taxes; establishing roots in America; and often doing menial labor work, to be honest, that most Americans don't want to do anyway. In addition, the labor work many immigrants are willing to do usually takes place in residences all across the country. Immigrants blend into American households, playing vital roles in housekeeping, cooking, child care, landscaping, and all the other functions that keep our homes running smoothly. Many immigrants are essential parts of our family units, keeping life running at home so we can go out and pursue our own American dreams: working outside the home, climbing the corporate ladder, creating jobs, pumping money into the economy. . .

Only when we understand how vital immigrants are to our lives do the political talking points and propaganda become personal. These are real human beings, not cold hard statistics; mowing our lawns, doing our laundry, taking care of our children, cleaning our offices at night while we sleep, picking the fresh produce that we enjoy from the supermarket, and preparing our meals when we dine at restaurants. The story of coming to America and starting a new life is no longer just about the dreams of the immigrants. Their story is now essential to the success of our own. It is woven tightly into our families, our hopes, and our dreams for the future.

If we don't learn to see the human stories behind the talking points, we will keep chasing our tails forever. We will keep going in circles, recycling the same conversations and propaganda for years to come, and nothing will ever be solved. Is that what we really want as our country's legacy—a reputation of being unable to maintain the integrity of one of the very pillars we were founded upon?

#3: They're here to take, not to give.

Another set of falsehoods about immigrants is that they take more than they give: by not paying taxes, by depleting government services, and by taking jobs from American citizens. Like the other myths in this chapter, each of these is based on seeds of fear which, combined with ignorance and emotion, have been turned into talking points and spread virally throughout the population. Nobody wants to be shortchanged, especially in his or her own native country. It's unreasonable, however, to jump to hysterical conclusions that immigrants are paying fewer taxes than you are, taking your job, and taking government benefits away from you. In fact, the opposite is true; these individuals make many consistent and valuable contributions like these to our infrastructure.

Revenue: Undocumented immigrants pay taxes just like the rest of us, including payroll taxes (billions of dollars into social security alone), sales tax, and property tax (whether indirectly as renters, or directly as homeowners). They contribute to economic growth with the purchasing power gained from their labor. The overall effect is that rather than taking from our workforce and economy, they actively feed it. In 2013 alone, undocumented immigrants added over $31 billion into the American economy.

Employment: Studies show that, rather than taking American jobs, unauthorized workers actually complement the skills of American workers. For example, when immigrants contribute to the growth of industries like retail, agriculture, landscaping, and hospitality, more middle-class jobs are created in management, design and engineering, accounting, marketing, and other highly skilled areas. Statistics show that there's no correlation between unemployment rates and the arrival of newcomers.

Government services: Undocumented individuals give more, through taxes and labor, than they receive in any sort of benefits from the federal government. In fact, they don't even qualify for services that many Americans take for granted, like welfare, food stamps, Medicaid, or other public benefits. In addition to not taking from our government services, immigrants are active contributors through payroll taxes, infusing $183 billion into Medicare funds between 1996 and 2011, and paying $13 billion into Social Security annually.[5]

When facts like these cut through the fear, ignorance, hysteria, and misinformation, it is easy to see the truth. As a whole, immigrants are driven to America by a hunger to contribute their talents to our country and succeed; and they give much more than they receive.

#4: Their names tell the whole story.

Our ignorance is rarely more on display than when we make snap judgments about a person based on their outward appearance. Let's

---

5   "Giving the facts a fighting chance"; American Immigration Council, Special Report 2015.

be honest, someone who looks or sounds Hispanic or Latino, is more frequently attached to the stereotype of a "typical immigrant," and assumed to be guilty of the very myths being discussed.

For instance, you may have seen a controversial news story about a couple that, rather than tipping their server, left her a hateful message instead—presumably because of her ethnicity. The server's name was Sadie Karina Elledge, eighteen years old, Latina by heritage, and an American citizen. She had recently graduated high school, was waitressing for work and was headed off to community college, when she received this message on her customers' receipt, in lieu of a tip: "We only tip citizens."

This story circulated like wildfire on social media. I'll admit it—reading this felt like a punch in the stomach for me, as a Latina-American and as a mom. I thought of how I would feel if that happened to my daughter; if someone looked at her and saw only her "label" and nothing else. My blood began to boil—and I wasn't alone. Sadie's grandfather, an attorney with his own law firm, posted a photo of the receipt to Facebook with some choice words for his granddaughter's customers. He also told the proud story of his bicultural family (Honduran and Mexican), including his American (citizen) grandchildren. The grandfather also noted that, in their thirty years living in Virginia (the American south by geopolitical standards) his family has rarely run into discrimination.

We have, living among us, working, paying taxes, and contributing to society, people from a large variety of countries all over the world. While it's true that the statistical majority come from Mexico, just because someone looks or sounds Hispanic does not mean they are Mexican—and even if they are Mexican, this does not mean they are an illegal immigrant. The fact that we are in 2016 and the general public still needs education on the difference between culture and citizenship is stunning to me. I've asked this question before, but it warrants repeating: Have we really made progress as an open-minded, tolerant, diverse country? Or is this type of ignorance in the minority? If we ignore it enough, will it go away on its own? My concern is, that if it hasn't gone away yet—what will it take?

#5: They don't love America.

Yet another persistent myth is that immigrants are not as patriotic as native-born citizens. One of the most definitive piece of evidence that exists to contradict this, is their selfless service in our very own military. This includes undocumented people, who will actually lie just for the opportunity to serve in our country.

This precedent of foreign-born residents serving in our military dates back to the 1840's, when they made up *half of all military recruits.* 20% of the 1.5 million-member Union Army during the Civil War were immigrants.[6] Many have also fought in modern wars, including in Vietnam. As of 2015, 65,000 green card holders served in the US military.[7] The number of documented individuals serving and dying for our country is much higher, in the hundreds of thousands.

The hunger for a better life that drives immigrants to America also feeds an unconditional love and pride for their new country. As far as embracing your culture and country is concerned, I cannot think of a more patriotic way to do that than by defending it with your life. If you really want to judge a person's commitment to their

---

6   MigrationPolicy.org. "Immigrants in the US Armed Forces." May 15, 2008. http://www.migrationpolicy.org/article/immigrants-us-armed-forces

7   Pbs.org. "They served their country. Now they can't live in it." September 10, 2015. http://www.pbs.org/newshour/updates/served-country-now-cant-live/

country, see if they are willing to die for it. A willingness to make the ultimate sacrifice is the ultimate commitment.

So, how do we repay them? By sending the undocumented ones back to their country when their service is complete: separating them from their families, putting them back on the waiting list, treating them like second class citizens, discriminating against them for how they look and sound, and denying them essential government services. We tell them, through our actions—"You can die for us, but we won't lift a finger for you." How is that fair? Is that the face of humanity and democracy?

CLOSING ARGUMENT

An immigration system serves many purposes. It creates a path to citizenship for those who truly want a new life for themselves and their children. It invites talents, ambitions, and skillsets into a country, ultimately strengthening that country's economy. It brings in revenue and resources, and contributes to our government and armed forces.

A good immigration system also helps control a country's borders. When regulated properly—inviting in the good people and keeping out the bad—a process of admitting new citizens strengthens a country's identity and core values. A country that does not protect its borders, culture, and identity will ultimately become a different country. A sensible set of border controls and citizenship laws, therefore, is one of a nation's most important functions to secure its future.

Is it any wonder that immigration is one of the most complicated, convoluted, and controversial issues facing America today? With a country of our size, population, economic and military power, and spirit, this is not at all surprising. While the laws and technicalities of immigration are beyond most ordinary citizens' control, there is something we each can control. Each one of us has the power to get educated on the facts vs. the stereotypes and outright lies. We can make the decision to fight for change in the system, rather than punishing those victimized by it.

The majority of immigrants are well-intentioned individuals with a hunger to achieve something better in life than their current circumstances will allow. They're not conniving, evil criminals trying to trick us or take something away from us. In fact, most of them are trying to give something back to us in exchange for an opportunity to succeed. Through their passion and willingness to move mountains, immigrants remind us of our best qualities. They serve as walking pages of American history, glimpses of a time when their contributions would have been celebrated, not shunned. The first step in returning to that time is the decision to fix the process—not punish the people in it.

VERDICT

Although I was born here, I, like many other Americans, come from immigrant parents. Unless you are Native American, you do too—whether that means going back hundreds of years or just one or two generations. Nearly every American Dream began with someone born someplace other than America, who made the decision to come here. Never take that for granted; never forget the sacrifices that were made on your behalf, even well before you existed. As a country, our successes stand on the shoulders of the sacrifices of immigrants.

And so next time, when anybody wants to tell you they want to build a "wall" on our border, remember behind that wall is struggle, determination, hunger. Behind that wall, could be the next cure for cancer, the next scientist, the next artist, the next drummer, the next anything they work hard enough to become!

—Camila Cabello

5

CANCER

I know you are asking today, "How long will it take?" Somebody's asking, "How long will prejudice blind the visions of men, darken their understanding, and drive bright-eyed wisdom from her sacred throne?" Somebody's asking, "When will wounded justice, lying prostrate on the streets of Selma and Birmingham and communities all over the South, be lifted from this dust of shame to reign supreme among the children of men?" Somebody's asking, "When will the radiant star of hope be plunged against the nocturnal bosom of this lonely night, plucked from weary souls with chains of fear and the manacles of death? How long will justice be crucified, and truth bear it?"

—Martin Luther King, Jr.,
Selma to Montgomery March address

On March 7, 1965, one of the bloodiest and most tragic events in American history unfolded in Selma, Alabama. It was called "Bloody Sunday."

Despite repeated attempts by African Americans of the town of Selma to become registered to vote, only two percent of the applicants actually made it onto the polls. A protest was organized and the participants decided to march fifty miles from Selma up to the state capitol in Montgomery. They never made it across the Alabama River, the body of water which runs through Selma. State and local police blocked them on the Edmund Pettus Bridge. The scene was beyond ugly: white police attacking black marchers in a cloud of tear gas.

No matter your color, culture, political leanings, pride for this country . . . if you really believe in what America stands for, picturing that scene should make you cringe. It goes against who we are.

But the question is: have we learned any lessons from Selma and so many other civil rights incidents from our past?

Look at news stories from the current chapter of American history—Ferguson, Baltimore, Dallas, New Orleans, and Charlotte. The trigger may have changed; instead of voter rights, it is now perceived racism towards African Americans amongst police officers. But the way the scenes are playing out feels like déjà vu: protesters and police officers in riot gear squaring off in the middle of American streets, sometimes with tear gas and other riot deterrents, and tragically, sometimes with deaths and grievous injuries on both sides. Blood is still being shed in our streets; children are losing their parents; and it doesn't appear that there's a solution in sight.

But are things as bad now as they were when the civil rights movement was just growing its roots? Are they better? Or are they worse? We like to believe the narrative that we're always making progress. As individuals, as a society, and as a nation, we're learning, growing, evolving, and becoming better each day. But when it comes to living with each other side by side in a mix of ethnicities, backgrounds, and cultures, it doesn't *seem* like we're doing any better than that bloody day in Selma. It doesn't seem like we've learned anything at all. As generations continue to pass by, and the same headlines seem to be repeating themselves—are we on course to leave the same set of problems for our own kids? Sadly, I believe we are.

Because to me, racism is a disease: a sick and twisted plague that we are left without a cure for, even so many years later. Looking at someone from the outside and having hateful thoughts materialize inside your head—this is a mental cancer, spreading cell by cell throughout our culture with each hateful thought, word, and act. Protests like the one in Selma may be a symptom, but behind every march, every demonstration and every uprising, there is a full-fledged disease lurking and festering in the background.

Disease (n): a problem that a person, group, organization, or society has and cannot stop

Well over a decade into the 21st century, racism is still a problem that society cannot appear to stop. Here we are, still discussing the issue of this powerful, sickening hatred toward people of other ethnicities. This hatred has permeated into all areas of our society. Malignant racial tumors are popping up all over the place, and we read about them in headline after headline.

There's the story of alleged racism in the US Army—where one day is set aside for soldiers to be as racist as they want toward each other. *As racist as they want.* Think about that. In itself this implies that people naturally *want* to be racist, to be hateful and bigoted toward others. It assumes that as human beings, we naturally have this disease inside of us, just dying to be unleashed; that we can't help ourselves. It implies that we *want* to hate each other, and the only thing stopping us is society. It's out of our control, an incurable disease, and we are the helpless victims.

Another nasty, malignant tumor popped up in the University of Oklahoma fraternity that was kicked off campus when a video surfaced of the fraternity brothers *on their way to a leadership event* performing a racist chant. The chant was allegedly a routine piece of the fraternity's pledge initiation process. It was familiar and apparently, nobody thought twice about doing it. The University president said he did not believe the young men involved were "racist in their hearts." In this case, was the tumor so invisible that nobody saw it? Are we so used to living with racism in America that we barely notice it anymore? An untreated cancer is even deadlier. When we pretend it doesn't exist, it always finds a way of rearing its ugly head.

COURT OF PUBLIC OPINION: THE BALTIMORE BAND-AID

Even when we do acknowledge that it exists, how are we treating the cancer of racism in America? The overwhelming solution at the moment is to protest. When done rationally and for the right reasons, protests have historically led to positive social change. Today's civil rights protests, however, are morphing into a far more insidious and far less productive phenomenon—a misguided type of social activism. A social activism that reacts before researching. A social activism that marches before it has a meaning for doing so. A social activism that screams before it listens to reason. A social activism that creates the illusion that something has been solved.

In 2015, the Baltimore City State's Attorney s office charged six police officers in the death of Freddie Gray, an African American man who died from a severe spinal injury while being transported to jail in the back of a police van. Three of the officers involved were Caucasian, and three were African American. One officer was a woman newly promoted to sergeant; a few were rookies; and one was an experienced lieutenant with 17 years on the force. When the arrests of the officers were announced, people of Baltimore who had only recently left the streets after protesting the death of Freddie Gray rushed back onto the streets to celebrate. They felt vindicated, even though nothing had actually been proven or disproven in a court of law. But the celebration would end quickly because, even though we will never know what really happened to Freddy Gray, the legal outcome was that there was no evidence of wrongdoing on the part of the officers.

"No evidence of wrongdoing" is not to be confused with innocence. In situations like these, there is no "innocent" vs. "guilty." It's never that clear, especially when the situation results in death. Something bad went down that day. Only the people involved will ever know what exactly happened and which party was responsible for it. But the law looks at charges and accusations, and ultimately determines whether there's enough evidence to convict based on the charges filed. Unfortunately, we may not always agree with the final decision.

In Baltimore, hints of disagreement began on day one, when many believed that the City State's Attorney's office acted prematurely in light of the deep divide between the police and the community stemming from alleged charges of police brutality. Why else would charges be brought up so quickly? Some people speculated that the top legal office was trying to make "the problem" go away as quickly as possible, and avoid tensions in the community.

What they (and we, the public) didn't count on was that the problem of police brutality wouldn't go away that easily. With nobody found definitively "guilty" and nothing legally resolved, the case would essentially be left open—like a wound left to fester. The rotting wound of distress, resentment, and hate that was opened in Baltimore has since dominated storylines involving police and the community. Why? Because this case, and others like it, are tried incessantly in the court of public opinion.

This is a "court" bearing little resemblance to our actual legal process. Its trials are based on hearsay, rumors, speculation, and each person's individual legal opinion (whether expert or, more often, not). Fueling it all is the widespread belief that few Americans ever get a fair trial.

After Baltimore, the court of public opinion began holding trials in other American cities whenever people were dissatisfied with the legal outcome of a case. In Ferguson, Dallas, New Orleans, Minneapolis, Charlotte, and other cities, the media and social media alike announced "cop kills unarmed man" and the people rushed to the streets with signs and voices raised in anger, immediately convicting the police and demanding instant justice for the victim— before finding out any of the facts.

The frustration and confusion are understandable. When we see yet another story about another black man being killed by a police officer, how can we not question what's really happening? We see the same pattern, the same basic plotline playing out over and over, in city after city, and our emotions drive us into a sense of social justice. We want answers. But are we allowing our frustrations to overtake the legal process?

Watching these stories play out, the basic principle of "innocent until proven guilty" is becoming a casualty of social activism. Judging people in the court of public opinion instead of in an actual court of law is a slippery slope that will be difficult, if not impossible, to climb back up. Our democratic legal process is one of the greatest things about our country. Is this often-combustive passion we are now demonstrating as a nation putting our legal process in jeopardy? By the time any of these controversial cases goes to a jury trial, there are few people who haven't heard "all" the details of the case via social media, and formed their opinion about it based on that "expert" point of view. The death of unbiased opinions appears to be a direct casualty of this new form of misguided social-media activism.

Continuing to use Baltimore as an example: was anything really solved there? Or was how we handled the death of Freddy Gray merely a template for future police shootings? It seems that Baltimore was the beginning of a dangerous new "normal," which subsequently spread to other cities where social-media activism has taken hold.

The incidents in these cities have shown us that this type of activism isn't ending the violence. Nor is it stimulating honest conversations. I believe that the goal of true social activism is to move us forward toward a solution. But this version of it—this anger-laced, bitter, confrontational version—is moving us backward. Each time we go through this, no winner is declared, and we only become more frustrated, angry, and divided.

It seems to me that the only thing today's riots do is to make matters even uglier. How can we honestly seek out a solution if we're trapped in our tunnel vision: taking revenge on the person or people proven guilty in the court of public opinion? It seems as if today's activism is about avenging actions, instead of about making progress. It's about punishing rather than solving, and dividing rather than unifying.

This isn't working. It's not bringing us together. If the protests, riots, blaming, and punishments aren't solving the problem, what's the point? The band-aids aren't sticking. The tension is building. When we try to catch the "rogue racist," punish him or her, and then move on, pretending the problem ended with that sole person, we make the problem worse. We create more tension. All this social-media activism is doing is making us more bloodthirsty for revenge, programming us to demand it as a pressure valve to release our racial tensions.

The cancer is spreading, and the prognosis is grave. We're losing sight of a lasting, long-term cure. We're forgetting the message of a certain great man who had a dream, and not a short-term one of social activism and feel-good Band-Aids. No, this man had a dream for change so powerful, and so real, that it would last for lifetimes and beyond.

THE POWER OF A COMMUNITY

It has been 54 years since Martin Luther King, Jr. stood on the steps of the Lincoln Memorial and gave his infamous "I Have a Dream" speech. On August 28, 1963, King addressed approximately 250,000 people who had gathered on the mall in Washington, with millions more watching on television. I think of all that has changed since then—in science, technology, and medicine, with many advances that have made our lives better—but here we are, still arguing about racism after all these years. The protests-turned-riots, the racism, the violence, Americans fighting Americans over skin color and ethnicity—that has not changed. We need to find a solution, because these are the fundamental pieces of the puzzle that have to be properly set in order for us to find true unity under one American identity.

Was this Martin Luther King's dream—that all these years later we would still be searching for these missing pieces? That we would be fighting the same battles he did? That there would still be blood shed in American streets in the name of skin color? I don't think this was his dream—I think this was more like his nightmare, the American nightmare. We are doing exactly what he told us *not* to do. Would Dr. King be proud, watching citizens destroy their own neighborhoods? The answer to this question can be found in King's own words on the subject, from a speech he gave at the American Psychology Association's annual convention in Washington DC in September of 1967:

> Urban riots must now be recognized as durable social phenomena. They may be deplored, but they are there and should be understood. Urban riots are a special form of violence. They are not insurrections. The rioters are not seeking to seize territory or to attain control of institutions. They are mainly intended to shock the white community. They are a distorted form of social protest.[8]

All in all, King approached the subject with exactly this type of education and understanding of the core issues at play, while also

---

8   http://www.motherjones.com/politics/2015/04/what-martin-luther-king-thought-about-urban-riots

remaining consistent with his views on nonviolence. While he did disagree with rioting as a means to an end, he also acknowledged that riots frequently resulted from the long-term mistreatment of a community.[9] I see his point of view as a common sense one, and I also agree that rioting can result from years of pent-up emotion and frustrations. This is understandable, and when a community is outraged, I support the right of that community to protest—as long as it's peaceful. People have a fundamental need to make their voices heard. It's when protests turn into riots that I put my foot down.

I cannot agree with or support people who hurt their own community in the name of anger. Pretending that a riot is for the benefit of the community is nothing but an excuse to destroy property. In Baltimore, the price tag on that destruction was roughly $9 million, which included damage and destruction to 284 businesses and two homes. A true community does not use anger as an excuse to destroy itself. Instead, it sticks together, despite the anger and frustration, and follows the same basic rules of life and common sense: respect, kindness, teamwork, and camaraderie, especially in difficult times. People looking to improve their communities exemplify these qualities.

In the midst of the volatility of the riots in Baltimore, community members stepped up, and they did so in a powerful, positive way. A now-iconic photograph taken by photojournalist Van Applegate shows a line of brave African American men, standing shoulder to shoulder in the middle of a city street, acting as a human barrier. Arms folded in strength and unity, and with gazes fixed forward, these men stood strong. They were not standing in protest against the police. No, they were protecting the police in their community from

9   http://time.com/3838515/baltimore-riots-language-unheard-quote/

their own neighbors who might wish to cause harm. And in turn, they protected the angry protestors from letting their emotions turn to physical violence (with potentially severe consequences). Those men stood in solidarity in the middle of that street, protecting their entire community.

The photograph gives me chills to this day, because it shows the true power of humanity, the power of community. Those men demonstrated real power and strength, as opposed to the rioters, who gave in to weakness by burning down homes and businesses and terrorizing their own community. The men in the photo stood together against that weakness.

This photo still inspires me, and I want my daughter and her generation to be just as inspired. Is it too idealistic to wish that all communities will form one giant line of strength and unity, especially when it seems like the hardest possible choice? When the easy decision is to divide against each other and rebel, this is exactly when we must find strength in unity. When the fires are raging and the smoke is burning our eyes, and we can't see clearly, this is the exact time that we must find our way to the high road and come together powerfully and positively. At this summer's Democratic National Convention, First Lady Michelle Obama said, "When they go low, we go high." This phrase became a motto for the election. Regardless of political affiliations, we should extend this sentiment beyond the election—especially when current events threaten to bring us down. That's when we need to come together and find a way to rise above.

That's how community should work: people coming together, especially in times of divide, and standing together in a powerful wall of unity. Anyone can light a match, especially in the middle of a fire. It takes courage and humanity to walk boldly into the middle of the fire, take a stand, and attempt to extinguish it without regard for one's own safety. When we all choose to do that—when we all decide to selflessly and humanely do the right thing together, on behalf of our collective community—that's when we will have one, United, States of America.

CLOSING STATEMENT

In March 2015, you may recall that Starbucks tried to inspire a national conversation about racism. Starbucks baristas were instructed to write the words "Race Together" on coffee cups. The idea was to encourage customers to see those words, and spontaneously start a conversation about race relations in America.

According to the Starbucks employee memo on the issue, the company was hoping to foster empathy and common understanding in the country, to do its part as the country faced ongoing racial tension, and to promote awareness and understanding through real efforts to have conversations and share information about the issue of racism.

Think about some of those goals in relation to the conversations in this chapter. Since March 2015, have we moved closer or further away from empathy and common understanding? Have racial tensions decreased or increased in America? Are we having open "dialogues" more or less often?

At the time, Starbucks was mostly mocked and criticized for its "Race Together" initiative. People joked about how overly simplistic it seemed, to believe that Starbucks would solve one of our most pressing social issues over cups of coffee. We were all cynical, asking if this was nothing more than a publicity stunt. What did they expect to really happen as a result?

One week into the experiment, Starbucks issued another memo stating that its baristas would stop writing "Race Together" on people's cups. They would go back to just serving coffee again, but they hoped that the conversation about race in America would continue on.

I will admit that I was amongst the doubters at the time. But now, in retrospect, I understand why Starbucks was the perfect place to start that conversation. If you think about it, the coffee chain is a level playing field, attracting the most blended customer base of possibly any brand today. People of all heritages, cultures, jobs, and walks of life converge at their local Starbucks each morning to stand and wait *together* for their names to be called out. Being social is literally written into your coffee order, and now *everybody knows your name.*

For anyone trying to encourage strangers into an honest conversation, wouldn't this type of social, conversational, friendly atmosphere be a dream come true? Perhaps Starbucks was only trying to remove the discomfort of an uncomfortable conversation, by putting it onto one of the most non-threatening objects possible: a cup of coffee.

I see now that Starbucks tried to shine a spotlight on the elephant in the room, which few people were (and still are) willing to acknowledge. The company's intention to address the issue openly and proactively was an honorable one. Especially now that we have seen what has happened since: how the issue of racism has exploded violently into our lives, well beyond coffee counters and news headlines. The conversation has now spilled over into the streets in the form of riots, online in social media battles, into living rooms, at professional sporting events (with football players sitting and kneeling during our national anthem), and in many other places in our everyday lives. It is quite clear that the elephant in the room is stomping his giant feet, refusing to be ignored. If we don't at least attempt to have an honest discussion, tensions will only continue to bubble up in communities all across America.

It might sound crazy for me to say this, but did we blow a golden opportunity to address those tensions in a calm, civilized conversation over coffee? If you think about it, the only conversations we're having now about discrimination come in the wake of those protests, marches, and riots. Unfortunately, the conversations end up being more about the violence than about the tensions fueling it. As a country, we seem to have trouble starting open, honest conversations about controversial topics.

It is difficult, if not impossible, to force people to break into spontaneous conversation about a sensitive topic—especially racism. When the headlines first came out about the "Race Together" messages being scribbled on customers' lattes, our collective cynical radar went off. We judged and opined quickly, without stopping to think first. Our instant verdict was that it was a forced conversation and the whole thing felt uncomfortable, so we went for the easy out and cracked jokes. It was ultimately much easier to mock the coffee chain than it was to think about the real issue. We wanted to feel comfortable again.

In our rush to go back to feeling comfortable, however, it seems we missed a key reality about controversial issues: When you ignore them, they don't go away. They remain just under the surface of our lives, growing more tense, like a giant elastic band stretching tighter and tighter, waiting to snap.

What is feeding this tension? What is stretching the elastic band? Well, for one thing: denial. In many people's minds, if a problem doesn't affect them, it's not a threat, and therefore it does not exist— like cancer. The thing about a cancer, whether physical or social, is that if it exists, you are never immune to it. If it's a threat to someone else, it can be a threat to you. It's disturbing that we can be in such denial that the problem still exists.

We're in denial about our diversity as a country, and that denial has led to ignorance of the problem. We're a veritable rainbow of racial diversity, but when we avoid the issues of racism and discrimination based on skin color, we're pretending that we're not diverse at all. We're pretending that we don't need to talk about the problem and that it will go away by itself.

The tension generated by our denial, our defensiveness, our silence, and our outright avoidance of the issue has festered into anger, bitterness, and resentment. The cancer is spreading. So what do we do about it?

We talk to each other. It doesn't have to be over a coffee at Starbucks, but it has to be somewhere. We need to release this tension and attack the cancer head on in order to have any hope of curing it. Our conversations might well be the cure.

The most effective conversations we will have with each other will not be forced, or contrived, or media-driven. The conversations that will create the most change will be the real ones that we have with each other, one-on-one. I believe it will be the personal, not public, conversations that matter in the long run.

VERDICT

We should try to find strength in our diversity—not use it as an excuse to turn on each other. We should seek out the power in our humanity, not the poison in our differences. Unfortunately, it seems like we have a long way to go to do that.

I received an email from an African American friend. She is an educated, successful woman who is also a talented, published author. When I read her email, my blood boiled.

> I was attacked this week on Twitter. A black lady that I follow tweeted a very positive quote with the hashtag "You're gonna be amazing." This is a saying that her mother always told her. I retweeted her post and responded to her. Some person I do not know saw our conversation and tweeted back to both of us "a n-word aint sh**" (except, they spelled both words out). I was hurt, but mostly angry. I thought about responding, but didn't for two reasons. First, sometimes silence is the best policy, especially when you are angry. Second, I thought about how that baseball player, Curt Schilling, found out

who bullied his daughter. If he can find that out, it can be reversed and someone can find information about me too. So, I let it wash off my back. At first, I wanted it deleted off my notifications page, then I thought, no, I'm glad it's there because whenever I look at it, I feel more ambitious and confident because I know it's a lie.

I think about how that ignorant, anonymous Twitter troll, hiding behind that cloak of anonymity, took one look at my friend and—without knowing a thing about her, just because of the color of her skin—made a hateful judgment about her. I think about it, and you know what? I feel tired. Tired of excuses, tired that we're still having this conversation. My father had to deal with bigotry back in the 1960s because of his accent, and my mother continues to struggle with the issue today due to her own heavy accent. Countless other Americans deal with it daily, like my friend fending off an online troll. Aren't you disgusted that we're still going around in circles like this; chasing our tails but not getting any closer to real solutions? I am, and I am disgusted.

As brilliant as we are as a society, we are regressing as human beings. We are losing our courage, our will to fight. We don't want to be bothered. We are no longer as willing to stand up as we once were. We are afraid to put our beliefs on the line and be judged. We are too concerned with protecting ourselves, our comfort zones, our egos, and our emotions. It's time to get uncomfortable, scratch the itch, and get outraged (in a productive way) that this is still happening after all these years. If we don't, this cancer will eat us all alive.

6

POLITICAL CORRECTNESS

Our lives begin to end the day we become silent about things that matter.
—Martin Luther King, Jr.

W hat's stopping us from having honest conversations and confronting controversial subjects head-on? What are we afraid of?

Part of the answer seems to be that we're afraid of offending people—of causing conflict through our words and ideas. As a country, we are cowering behind a wall of political correctness. We're playing defense to avoid causing offense. So the question becomes: how can we possibly have real conversations about the things threatening to rip apart our American identity, if we're constantly worried about being politically correct?

We hear the phrase "politically correct" in the media, and most of us have likely heard (or said) the phrase ourselves at some point. Therefore, when something is deemed "politically incorrect," whether it comes from a disrespectful or insensitive public comment or otherwise, the memos start flying and then someone calls the media. That's when the rest of us see stories about elementary school kids with plastic guns and "inappropriate" t-shirts, homeowner's associations forbidding residents to fly the American flag, who's allowed to use which bathroom, controversies about saying the Pledge of Allegiance, and other stories where someone becomes offended by someone else. If something is considered offensive or "politically incorrect," the gloves come off and there is hell to pay.

Merriam Webster dictionary defines "politically correct" (or "PC") as: "agreeing with the idea that people should be careful to not use language or behave in a way that could offend a particular group of people."

It seems, however, that the boundaries of this definition are constantly expanding to include anything that conveniently supports the narrative at hand. Slapping the "politically incorrect" label on somebody's words or actions just makes for a faster, more convenient verdict in the court of public opinion.

Beyond the public labels and media stories however, we are allowing this concept of political correctness to seep into our day-to-day personal mindsets. Its influence is more indirect now, than it was in the past, when one person would openly accuse another of being "politically incorrect" and a good old-fashioned debate would ensue. No, the new brand of political correctness is coming through as one-sided, fearful silence. It's as if we're so afraid of saying something potentially offensive, that we keep our mouths shut and move on. Our fear of offending others is leading to self-censorship.

This fear of being offensive, and the subsequent self-imposed silence of censorship concerns me, especially as the mother of a constantly curious, intelligent, perceptive adolescent daughter. I'm worried about the message this is communicating. Are we teaching the next generation to steer completely away from conflict and conversations that don't fit neatly in a politically correct box?

As parents, one of our jobs is to teach our kids to respect others, regardless of their opinions, gender, ethnicity, cultural identity, skin color, or sexual orientation. We do our best to protect them from harmful and hurtful thoughts, words, and ideas. But in our quest to do the right thing and raise our children to be decent human beings, I wonder if we've gone overboard. I wonder if this pursuit of political correctness is giving them the message to avoid uncomfortable conversations. I wonder if we're showing them, through our own actions, that the easier, safer path is to stay quiet and stick with the people and conversations that mirror their own points of view. Because of our own fear, are we teaching our children to replace a point of view with political correctness?

Here's an even bigger question to ask in the middle of this ongoing PC debate: Is political correctness even a real thing? Or is it nothing but an outdated, misunderstood phrase we're all still hiding behind, as a way of avoiding the uncomfortable but honest conversations about the issues that divide us as a country? Perhaps it was made up by people who get their feelings hurt easily to make us feel bad about ourselves if—God forbid—we say the wrong thing.

No matter where the truth lies, today political correctness quietly lurks beneath the surface of our conversations: If we say the wrong thing, if we step out of bounds, if we offend the wrong people, if we are even potentially politically incorrect, we will be called on it.

VERDICT

Quite frankly, if being "politically correct" is your reason to stay quiet and avoid confronting the real issues that are dividing us as a people, you're being intellectually lazy. You're either too lazy to learn about an issue enough to discuss it intelligently, or you mistakenly (and self-righteously) believe that being politically correct automatically makes you "right," and your opinions superior to those of everyone else.

What are you afraid of? Not understanding the issue? Research it. Being proven wrong? Get over it. You *will* be wrong some of the time. We all are. It's inevitable.

This is especially true because few issues are clear-cut, and certainly not as definitive as we're often made to think. There are always nuances, and the truth sits somewhere in the middle. Not all cops are racist, not all immigrants are criminals, not all gun owners are "gun nuts," not all Arabs are terrorists—and the list goes on.

When it comes to people's personal beliefs, we hold onto more fiction than fact. Therefore, even when people have the best intentions to be politically correct, it often backfires—because they're not basing that political correctness on fact. Maybe they're going along with the popular crowd, angling to fit in and be validated as "good people." Perhaps, in their eyes, being PC is the guaranteed way of being accepted—no questions asked.

But being politically correct is not a "get out of jail free" card. It is not a safety net to save you from having a challenging conversation or confronting a complicated issue. Being PC does not make you immune from controversy. Nor does being silent and denying that issues such as racism really exist in America. These are both the paths of least intellectual resistance.

The alternative path means becoming educated; thinking issues through from all angles; having the courage to be proven wrong or to possibly offend someone; and to potentially get lost in the gray area where there are no guaranteed right or wrong answers. Breaking away from the pack like this and thinking for yourself is the harder choice. It's the path of *most* intellectual resistance.

Does this path sound too hard for you? Maybe the mere thought of stepping away from the crowd, speaking up, and confronting a controversial conversation makes you want to crawl out of your skin with discomfort. Or perhaps you can see the benefits of taking such a risk anyway, even though it's difficult. ***Because, if none of us take any risks, how will we see any gains?***

We often talk about all the people who helped create America's great identity—and they did it one risk at a time. Our founding fathers, our immigrants, our civil rights leaders, and all the others who refused to stay silent; refused to be politically correct; and refused to take the path of least intellectual resistance. What each of these individuals did was difficult, and that's what made each of them great. That's how they shaped an entire nation: not through silence, but through their courage to speak up about the issues.

It's difficult to imagine that rebuilding and restoring our American identity by tackling hard topics of conversation won't challenge or offend at least a few of us. It might be a messy ordeal, and it certainly won't be quiet. But isn't the future of America worth it? The generations coming up now, including my daughter's generation, are watching us build a legacy we'll leave for them. They're watching us light the torch that they will ultimately have to carry.

What will the next chapter in our American story be, if this chapter ends with our inability to have a frank and honest conversation with one another? In the long run, isn't risking a little offense worth it in exchange for greatness?

7

CHANGEABLE STORIES

Once you touch the biographies of human beings, the notion that political beliefs are logically determined collapses like a pricked balloon.

—Walter Lippmann

We need to have the courage and willingness to explore, and talk to each other about, the most pressing and controversial ideas and issues dividing our country. What do the stories that we've covered reveal about who we are and who we want to be as an American people?

Well, when it comes to terrorists, we can't seem to agree on who the enemy is—let alone how to stay safe. To some of us, "America" is a bad word; we can't see past the things that embarrass

77

us about our country, and this blinds us to the things that make us proud of it.

When it comes to immigration, the fictional stories have out-shouted the factual ones, and we've lost sight of the honorable reasons people come to our country in the first place—and all the gifts they bring us.

Meanwhile, racism has developed into a cancer that, if we don't address it together (and soon), threatens to devour the diversity and uniqueness that America is supposed to represent.

In the middle of all these pressing issues, the more theoretical idea of political correctness has silenced many of us—and turned others into walking censorship monitors, dictating which ideas are offensive and which ones are safe for public consumption.

All of these stories and more are being narrated on the constantly updating, 24/7, all-seeing and all-knowing medium called the Internet. More specifically, those stories are coming alive on social media, where each person's version of the story, good or bad, right or wrong, is magnified. Through the relative anonymity of social media, each person is now granted a bully pulpit. Through their social media posts, those with strong opinions can now broadcast their message—which often comes across as "You either agree with me, or I will continue to pester and embarrass you until you see things my way." In the face of this relentless online bullying, it's no wonder that less outspoken people are simply going silent.

It's not surprising to me that the most important issues and stories dividing America are turning into one-sided conversations. What is the solution? What needs to happen for us to start talking *with* one another rather than *at* one another?

So far, the solution I've proposed is to get the facts, to research both sides of every story, to listen and learn and not be afraid to ask tough questions. Now, let's take this one step further. How can we dig deep and learn to understand where the person on the "other side" is *really* coming from in their arguments?

I realize that many of us believe we already know the answer to this question. If someone doesn't agree with us on an issue—if they don't see our side—there's an easy explanation: "They're an idiot. . . they're a liberal. . . they're a right wing conservative. . . they're a conspiracy theorist. . . they're brainwashed. . ." And sometimes the name-calling grows even more disgusting. Recall the racial slurs thrown viciously at my author friend via Twitter. I see these conversations playing out daily on social media and on the news, and I would imagine they're happening in homes, at work, and in schools too, on some level (although hopefully not as harsh). I see people talking to each other like this and ask: What's the point? What are we accomplishing here? It's as if we think that when someone disagrees with our point of view, they're doing it on purpose just to personally spite us.

The fact is: This name-calling and closed-mindedness is getting us nowhere. It's killing more conversations than it's starting. If we're going to make any kind of progress in coming together as a country, we need to put some thought into why we're behaving like this, especially in the face of disagreement. It begins with understanding *why* people believe the things they do.

Most people believe things for personal—not political—reasons. When we hold a strong belief about something, that belief is more likely to be rooted in a personal story, not a political viewpoint. What one side sees as insensitive, or wrong, or ignorant, is the other side's fierce commitment to the personal stories that drive their worldview.

How would that change these conversations for you, knowing that our political beliefs are driven by personal stories?

Here's an example of what I'm talking about: During the 2016 Republican National Convention in Cleveland, the stories we saw on the news were the typical media coverage. One after another, the talking heads pitted the right against the left, American against American. The coverage focused on political boxing matches, speculating on which candidate would "win" America. The convention, as well as the Democratic National Convention that would follow a week later in Philadelphia, was a perfect opportunity to stir the pot of division. At this point I think it's even safe to say that, based on your point of view, you know which cable networks are "safe" to watch so your opinion won't be challenged. Watching the media, we've become experts in listening only to the stories we agree with, and ignoring the rest.

Division and disagreement was the story inside the convention hall, anyway. *Outside* the building, one man decided to start a slightly different political conversation. Benjamin Mathes, a blogger, stood outside the RNC in the sweltering summer heat with a sign reading "Free Listening," and invited people to come over and say anything they wanted to him, without fear of judgment. He wrote an article about his findings, titled *How to Listen When You Disagree: A Lesson From the Republican National Convention.*

Most people who talked to Benjamin spoke about personal issues like their families, jobs, why they were attending the RNC, and probably even the weather. But that's not what his article was about. It was about a woman who walked over to him "like a young warrior preparing for battle" and announced that she was proudly pro-life. In her words, abortion is "wrong" and "people who have them should be arrested for murder." Benjamin, as he later revealed in his article, is pro-choice. But rather than judging or bullying her, he simply stood and listened instead. Then, he said something to her that I wish all Americans, especially those of us on social media, would say in the face of disagreement: *"Thank you for sharing that. Tell me your story. I'd love to know how you came to this point of view."*

So she did. The pro-life woman shared with the pro-choice man the personal story behind her belief: how all she ever wanted was to be a mother. But at 18, she was told that her ovaries were so damaged that she could never have children. She was most likely devastated in a way that most of us cannot imagine. Years of picturing herself bringing new life into the world, being a mother, raising children—all wiped out in a heartbeat. For her and others like her, "being a mother" went far beyond a medical diagnosis; it was a piece of her heart. Not every viewpoint about an issue is backed up by such a poignant personal story, but there is always a seed of personal belief behind what appears on the surface to be purely political.

Too many of us seem to be in denial about this—that there is even a small piece of personal perspective behind our political opinions. But can any of us honestly say that we *only* believe the things we do for political reasons? We like to think that, when it comes to anything political, our opinions are completely logical and based on the facts. This is part of the reason we've let emotionally divisive issues fester for so long. It's as if we're all sitting back and waiting for political solutions to our personal problems.

We're in denial about the fact that finding a personal reason to hate another human being is *far* from political. As far as I'm concerned, we can all talk about not "taking things personally" until we're blue in the face. But hate is personal.

This applies to so many of the topics in this book. Conversations that appear to be political on the surface almost always have a personal component. How could they not? "Terrorism" is something that directly affects the safety of your family, of your children. "Patriotism" is impacted directly by your family member, friend, or acquaintance who fought for our flag, and possibly was even injured or killed doing it. "Immigration," on a personal and universal level, is really a fear that the life you've worked so hard to build will somehow be threatened by a newcomer who doesn't share or understand your values. "Racism" is the fear that, if one group of people can be targeted with hate, what's to say that your community isn't next? Racism is not about hating "races," it's about people hating other people.

Do you think you're personally immune from hate? If you do, you are fooling yourself. You're forgetting that hate can be directed at any of us for any one of these reasons.

Let's not make the mistake of forgetting the humanity that is the common denominator of *all* these issues. Remembering the human element behind these "political" issues is the bridge that can bring us back together, beyond the politics and the "isms."

COURT OF PUBLIC OPINION

The conversations that the court of public opinion has labeled as "political" are actually extremely personal. These are human conversations with human consequences. Knowing that, my next question is: How do we start over? By "starting over," I mean hitting the reset button on all the emotions, the defensiveness, the denial, and the anger; re-learning how to actually talk *with* one another about the issues that affect us all. I'm talking about the return to common ground.

It starts with wanting to do better, and to be better participants in the conversation. Sometimes, being better begins with admitting that we have a problem. This was exactly the case when a white man called into a live C-SPAN television show where the subject of racial tensions was being discussed, and said something truly shocking to one of the show's guests, an African American woman and think tank president named Heather McGhee.

"I'm a white male and I am prejudiced," the caller said.

He went on to describe how his prejudice was something he had learned over the course of his life, reading story after story in the newspaper about young black males involved in crime. He talked about how reading all these stories crafted a certain narrative about black people in his mind. He said he was now afraid of the prejudice that had formed in his mind as a result, and finished his comment with a powerful question: "What can I do . . . to be a better American?"

In her detailed and thoughtful response, McGhee affirmed how powerful it is to be able to admit our prejudices, then seek to overcome them. She even offered the caller specific advice to help him reshape his beliefs about African Americans, particularly black males: "Get to know black families who are not involved in crime and gangs. . . turn off the news [which historically over-represents African American crime]. . . join a black or interracial church. . . read about the history of the African American community. . . foster conversation where you're asking exactly these kinds of questions."

What she was describing through those examples was a way in which a person can rewrite the personal story behind their beliefs. She was talking about how to give a personal story about prejudice a dramatically different ending. This is something, if we're willing, that each one of us can do. We can examine the true stories behind each of our beliefs; be willing to admit our stories are flawed, if that's the case; be open to a rewrite; and then change the endings to those stories. That is how we can all be better Americans.

CLOSING ARGUMENT

Can the stories behind a person's beliefs be changed? In the case of the man who called into that C-SPAN show, candidly admitting his prejudice, the answer apparently is "yes." Stories and beliefs *can* be changed, when the believer has the desire to change them.

But what about the people who seem to have unchangeable minds? I'm talking about the people who seem to be so set in their beliefs, one way or the other, that when someone dares disagree with them they fight back—and often viciously. Can their beliefs be changed? Or is it a lost cause to even try?

My daughter says we should forget about the people whose minds we cannot change, and concentrate on those who are open to discussion. She chimed in during a conversation about racism I was having with my collaborator on this book, who is around the same age and generation as I am. We were both sitting there, essentially eulogizing the future of America, feeling extremely pessimistic about the state of things in our country. We were commiserating about the division in our nation and asking: "Is there hope? Can people actually change their minds enough to come together and listen to each other?"

That's when Sofia walked into the room where we were working, and with all the casual perception that today's young people seem to have mastered, remarked that there will always be a percentage of people whose minds cannot be changed. She used an example from her own experience, of watching two people of different ethnicities trying to have a direct conversation about racism. In her example, one or both of the people were "totally racist" and the conversation was destined to end in anger—so why bother trying to have it? Why pick at a scab just for the sake of picking at it?

I thought about the two people in Sofia's example, reflecting that I've met people like the ones she described. The stories at the roots of their beliefs are so tightly woven into their worldview that to change them would be akin to pulling a loose string on a sweater. The whole thing might come undone (at least, that's the perceived risk). So, in Sofia's words, why waste your time on them when you can focus on the people who *do* have changeable mindsets?

As much as I completely understood what she was saying, I had (and still have) a hard time with it. But I don't blame my daughter for this, not in the least. Our kids, after all, learn much of what they believe by watching and listening to the adults around them. I had to wonder what message are we teaching our kids about confronting opposing viewpoints. Are we showing them that people's minds can't be changed, period, so why bother trying? If we are, and if we're also teaching them to fear the polarity of differing points of view and stay silent, then I believe the future of our American identity is in jeopardy. Specifically, I worry about the piece of who we are that's rooted in speaking our minds, not being afraid to disagree with our neighbors, and fighting for what we believe in. Does the next generation believe it's safer to stay silent and avoid rocking the boat—even if it compromises this vital piece of who we are?

This idea of giving up in the face of opposition really bothers me, especially because it came from my daughter. "Giving up" is not in our nature as Americans. Part of our identity has always been to fight, and fight hard, for what we believe in. We are a nation of fighters who don't just give up on something before we at least *try* to make it happen. There is a certain logic to saving our energy and focusing on the battles we have a better chance of winning. But as a country, have we ever gone after only the battles we were sure we could win? No. We've gone after the battles that needed to be fought, no matter how unchangeable the stories appeared to be. Many of them would have been considered losing battles from day one. We fought them anyway—because that's part of who we are. When we don't like the story being told, we get together and find a way to rewrite it.

Now, the story we are tasked with rewriting is the one of our identity moving forward. As the American people, who do we want to be? Will we be the people who remain silent in the face of opposition? Will we be the people who stick stubbornly to the stories that drive our beliefs, refusing to listen to others' views? Or, will we be the people who are willing to start honest (though potentially uncomfortable) conversations, and commit to seeing them through to a place of greater understanding?

Can the stories behind a person's beliefs be changed? The only way we'll ever find out is through our willingness to stop, listen, and learn from each other. Rather than continuously telling others how wrong they are, what if we get curious about each other's points of view instead? What if we say, like Benjamin Mathes did, "Thank you for sharing that. Tell me your story. I'd love to know how you came to this point of view." Story by story, one by one, we each have the power to change—or at least, respect—an unchangeable mindset.

VERDICT

A new, or newly rewritten, story needs a starting point. How about the choice to be better Americans? Being a better American means focusing on one common vision for the legacy of America.

To do that, we all need to make a choice. We need to decide what we want America to be, and what our priorities are. Will we prioritize the power of humanity and community over pointless, ego-driven battles where nobody wins?

These battles can only cease when we acknowledge that, on some things, *we might be wrong.* We might not have all our facts straight. We may be ignoring some personal stories underpinning our political beliefs. We might have to realize that the court of public opinion is a flawed way to discuss controversial issues, and come up with a better way of handling our frustrations. Left, right, and center, we might have to stop listening to only what we want to hear.

If we really want to create a better American legacy, we'll need to change some of the stories we've been telling ourselves.

8

PROVE THEM RIGHT

Here I am, the educator, trying to teach you the basics of life—good manners, values, morals, etc. And while I'm educating you, I'm reeducating and reawakening myself to the basics of my life. You, Sofia, are the only one who could do that for me. You have inspired me to look at myself and improve myself.

—**Cristina Perez**, *Living by Los Dichos:*
Advice From a Mother to a Daughter

The passage above is from my first book, a collection of life advice and personal stories grounded in Spanish proverbs called "Dichos." I intentionally structured *Living by Los Dichos* as lessons learned from my parents, which I then passed along to my daughter. She was three years old when the book was published, and she is now thirteen. I have watched the little girl, the tiny adorable inquisitive toddler, I wrote that book for, become a thoughtful, perceptive, and wise emerging adult. It is incredible to think that ten years have passed between then and now. Like any other mother, I am so unbelievably proud of the person that she is and continues to become—my heart overflows with pride and joy when I look at her!

Sofia continues to re-educate and reawaken me about life. This time around, during the writing of *Red, White, and Latina*, I'm proud to say that my daughter has been an active participant in the conversation. She has been an intelligent sounding board, a provider of thoughts and ideas, and a mini-focus group representing an entire future generation of Americans.

Because, truth be told, one of my greatest motivations for writing *Red, White, and Latina* is to give her and the next generations of Americans what they will need to carry the torch into our country's future. Our children are our legacy. They will define what America will become in the 21st century and beyond. They will determine whether America will be known for its unity, or for its division. They will decide whether people see us as a cultural world leader where people listen to, like, and respect each other and each other's differences—or if we will become a nation of embarrassment, where we can't stop bickering amongst ourselves long enough to lead the way in technology, medicine, humanity, and so on. Do we have what it takes to make America a positive role model once again? It is up to our future generations, starting with our own kids, to answer this question and to shape our legacy. Our American identity is in their hands.

This is a daunting, maybe even overwhelming mission for any generation to take on. Think about the Greatest Generation, was tasked with rebuilding America after so many of their young men were killed in World War II. But they persevered; worked hard; believed that America could return to its former glory; and, within a couple of decades, took that belief and flew it right to the moon. That generation of Americans was put to the test, and they demonstrated what they were made of. Is this next generation, my daughter's generation, up to the challenge?

My answer is absolutely "yes!" I know my daughter and her friends and classmates. I am around them all the time; I listen to their conversations and observe the way they approach life. They're smart enough to do it, and culturally diverse enough; collectively, they have multiple viewpoints on each issue; and they're not ashamed of their thoughts and feelings. From where I sit, they are possibly the most intuitive and authentic generation in history. They hold the power to blend intelligence, life experiences, authenticity, and cultural background into a solution that will empower us to embrace our differences. Right now, our differences divide us; we are stuck in an emotional stalemate where we are stuck in the idea of being "right." I believe the next generation will teach us how to listen to each other again.

To my daughter Sofia, to her friends, to your daughters and sons, to the upcoming generations tasked with starting a new conversation in America . . . here is my advice for you.

They're called trolls for a reason: Bullying in real life is bad enough, but when it goes undercover through the Internet, the volume goes up and the conversation can feel even more suffocating and personal. This is especially true in political and other divisive issues, where Internet bullies play on people's emotions and good hearts, trying to bait others into playing their games. The fact is that trolls are cowards, hiding behind the mask of anonymity and firing shots blindly at anyone who will listen. Stop listening to them! There are no arguments to be won, no honest and authentic conversations to be had, and nothing to be learned. Move on quickly before they tangle you up in their bully pulpit where you don't belong.

Don't rely solely on school to learn: The educational system is designed to teach you *how* to learn. It's up to you to figure out what you *need* to learn. Don't go to college for the sake of going to college. Instead, do your homework, research, figure out what you want to do in life, and then determine what you need to study to achieve that goal. Reverse-engineer your education: Decide where you want to go, and then chart a path to get there. Choosing your major and your future career is your first adult decision. Your education is an *investment* in yourself and your future, so choose carefully.

Then, no matter what you study, actively seek out new lessons that aren't covered in your books and in the classroom. Find out things that you can only learn by experiencing real life; by thinking through complicated issues; by talking to people who disagree with you and finding out the stories behind their beliefs; and by thinking about those hot-button topics from all sides. *Learn through living.* Take nothing at face value.

Work like your life depends on it: No matter how you personally arrived in America, put yourself in the shoes of those early Ellis Island immigrants. Pretend you're fighting to earn the right to stay in America. Take nothing for granted, especially the privilege of having a shot at capturing the American Dream. Each person that sets foot in America is faced with this question: "Now that I am here, what will I do here?" Whether you were born here or not, this question is yours to answer. The experience of your American Dream is personal and unique to you. It's your story: the story that will determine what you accomplish in your lifetime and the legacy you will leave behind.

Be curious, not confrontational: When you reject the need to prove yourself or be "right" and replace it with simple curiosity, you'll be surprised at what you can learn from someone else. Remember the man who stood outside the Republican National Convention and promised to listen, even when he disagreed to the core of his being with some of the things he was listening to. He took a deep breath, opened his ears, and chose to learn from others rather than confront them with why they were "wrong."

Redefine social activism: Remember the roots of positive, empowering change in America. Think of the greatest "activists" in history. Be aware of how they began by starting a peaceful conversation with the other side, and then took it from there. The great nonviolent activists didn't burn down businesses, raise their fists in violence, or attack people. They saw a cancer eating away at society; they stood up and said "this is wrong;" they protested peacefully to make their views heard; and they used their voices and words to communicate a solution.

Talk to people who disagree with you: Don't be afraid of the people who seem to have unchangeable mindsets. Behind what may seem like an entrenched, stubborn, misinformed opinion is usually a human being too afraid to change their mind about what they "know" to be true. The idea of changing your story can be a scary one. Start there, with that understanding. Show compassion and curiosity, and listen, even if you disagree. Above all, be kind. Learn how to express your political opinions and debate with respect and kindness, without trying to wound the other person.

Don't let the fear of being "politically incorrect" silence you: First and most importantly, always be respectful of others, regardless of how different they are from you. Disrespect is being intentionally unkind to another person. However, avoiding difficult conversations because of a fear of unintentionally offending someone is not a good plan. Research the issues, develop a point of view, and don't censor yourself—*especially* in the face of opposing points of view. Sometimes you'll be proven right; sometimes you will learn something new and change your point of view. By having the courage to speak up and taking a chance at being proven wrong, you are contributing to a stronger, more resilient, and honest American identity.

Wear it proud: Never let anyone make you feel like you have to choose between your cultural identity and your patriotism and pride as an American. You will come up against many compromises in life, some at work and some at home. This is not one of them. It is your right *and* responsibility to wear your culture and your patriotism with nothing but pride.

This is where things come full circle for me, after first writing a letter to my daughter in my book 10 years ago. Here is a letter in response, from my amazing daughter Sofia to all of us, with her take on the future of America.

Every Friday, my eighth grade history class has a discussion about a current events topic. We all get an article to read in advance, and we make up questions based on what was most interesting to us and things that the article made us think about. We have discussed immigration, the presidential election, Syrian refugees, and even the football player Colin Kaepernick.

Our discussions are normally really calm, civil, and productive, without a whole lot of emotion. We all discuss all sides of the issue, even the ones that people may personally disagree with. Sometimes, kids will even change their minds when they hear a new viewpoint on a topic that they hadn't considered before. One of my classmates did this the other day, saying, "I guess that makes sense." If we're wrong, we're willing to admit it and look at the other side of the argument. Even when some of the conversations continue outside the classroom afterwards, there's no yelling and screaming. We're still civil towards each other.

Then, after school, when I get home and find my mother watching the news or political coverage, I'm always surprised at how different the same exact discussions look when adults have them. I watch some of them yelling and screaming, turning red in the face, and banging the news desks as they argue. It's ironic that the adults are the ones screaming and yelling, while a bunch of eighth grade kids have a calm, civilized discussion. I can't imagine one of the members of the television media ever saying, "I guess that makes sense" and changing their mind. Nobody ever seems to change their mind on TV and I don't see many civil conversations happening.

If we kids can be civil, why can't adults? I mean, we're talking about the exact same current events topics as you are, the most controversial, emotional, ones. Shouldn't the conversation be the same?

This election year has been a great example of one big yelling and screaming conversation between Americans. First you have the voters focusing only on each candidate's flaws instead of their best qualities. It's like nobody realizes that even politicians are human beings and human beings have flaws. Nobody's looking at the whole picture. Then, you have the media making it worse because they're altering the original story. They're not telling the truth because if they were, we would see the bigger picture. The media tells people to focus on one thing, like emails, so people ignore stories about women being sexually harassed. The point is, they tell us where to look, and we put blinders on to everything else. We need to learn to listen and pay attention better or the media and politicians will keep twisting stories around and we won't know the difference, so we'll keep yelling and screaming at each other.

Finally, here's my advice to my fellow Americans: Cooperate. You need to find a way to cooperate with each other even if you don't have the same idea or opinion. If you don't cooperate nobody's ever going to come to a decision about how to fix these issues, ever. You're just going to yell and scream about the same things forever, and nothing will ever change.

To the politicians, stop making plans about what you want to do, and actually do something. To the candidates in future elections, start telling the truth. To the media, stop changing the facts of the story just to get ratings. To all of them and everyone else, find a way to have "political conversations" while being civil and cooperating. If you can't cooperate, you'll never be able to do anything.

Sofia Gonzalez
Age 13, November 2016

CLOSING THOUGHTS

We all have the privilege of walking in the footsteps of great Americans every single day. We are living in the looming shadows of our forebears. These early arrivals gave up everything to come to America and carve out better existences than the ones they'd had before. They gave up the only lives they knew in their home countries, sometimes gave up their educations and degrees, and often took unspeakable trips to get here. Once they hit American soil, they then did whatever it took— for however long it took—to stay here and succeed. They did all this because they believed it was worth it: that all their sacrifices paled in comparison to the promise of the American Dream. But despite their optimism, they were not blind.

When those weary travelers looked up at the Statue of Liberty, they had no delusions that she was perfect. They knew she had her flaws, but they believed her beauty outweighed her imperfections. They knew the risks, but saw the opportunity. They chose to come here anyway—and more like-minded people continue to make the same choice each day, arriving in what they believe to be the greatest country in the world. Their choice to come here, past and present, is sewn into the stars and stripes of our American flag.

Our national past also includes a group of people who had no choice but to come here. Slaves are rarely mentioned in this conversation, most likely because they did not make the voluntary decision to come to America. Yet they were still forced to give up the only lives they knew. The definition of an immigrant is somebody who relocates to a new country, and slaves are people who came to our country against their will. These were human beings offered no legal rights. They were ripped from their homes, separated from their families, forced to leave their countries, crushed and chained together like animals experiencing the unspeakable horrors of slave ships, and forced to work. These people were treated as less than complete human beings—they were treated as property. It is still chilling to me to think of this embarrassing chapter of our country's history, filled with personal stories of suffering created by our ignorance.

To be clear, I am not confusing people who voluntarily come to America with slaves who were forcibly brought here. The parallel I am making is about the inherent contributions of both groups of people, and about the reality that America was never perfect. A large and important piece of our American identity is African, including culture, music, foods, the arts, history, activism, and much more. Slavery left an indelible mark on our immigrant history, and when we forget that, we fail in our recognition of our own history and diversity—as well as the reality of what some have sacrificed for this nation.

It is our job, and especially the job of the next generation, to honor the incredible sacrifices of all Americans. For the ones who believed that America is worth the struggle, we must prove them right. We must prove to them that we understand why they did it. We must see in ourselves what they saw in us all along. We must show, through the legacy we create, that we are capable of embracing our flaws and our greatness together.

It is my hope that our children, after watching us pull away from each other, can learn what is needed to come back together. The torch will soon be in their hands. Our American identity hangs in the balance. Will our next chapter be an ending, or a new beginning?

Epilogue

GOING NUCLEAR

We cannot change the past, but we can change our attitude toward it. Uproot guilt and plant forgiveness. Tear out arrogance and seed humility. Exchange love for hate—thereby, making the present comfortable and the future promising.

—Maya Angelou

When I began writing this book, it was the summer of 2016, right after the national political conventions where the two major parties officially selected their candidates. The election year was already on fire by then, with friends, co-workers, families, neighbors, and total strangers fighting each other online and in person. It was disgusting, disrespectful, and downright embarrassing to watch. I didn't think it could get worse. I was wrong.

Next week, we vote for our next president. Summer has turned to fall, and while temperatures have cooled, the national political conversation has not. What began as a political debate—albeit a nasty one—has given way to something far more personal and (in my opinion) well beyond "normal" political character assassinations.

The election has turned into a publicly embarrassing competition to see who can shout the biggest lies the loudest. The audacity of the bully has been collectively accepted by America. Voters are being bombarded with sensationalistic "facts" about the candidates, along with fear mongering; each side insists that the other must be "stopped" or we're all doomed. According to a survey by the American Psychological Association, almost half of Americans have reported symptoms of severe anxiety as a result of election stress. Many people have reported simply unplugging to keep their sanity—turning off the television, going offline, and getting as far away from the political battles as they possibly can.

I don't blame those people as I sit watching the election coverage—watching both sides go for blood, without any apparent concern about the language being used to make their points. Where did all the hate come from? During the time I've written this book, that language has gone from nasty to downright nuclear.

I first used the phrase "going nuclear" in my second book (*It's All About the Woman Who Wears It: 10 Laws for Being Smart, Successful and Sexy Too*) while offering up various bits of life advice, particularly regarding relationships. One of my "marriage laws" warned couples against "going nuclear" when arguing—firing at each other with intensely personal, stinging words of war meant to wound. There are some things vicious enough that, once they are said, they cannot be taken back.

Similarly, I believe that some of the bitter and vile language we're being exposed to is not language we will be able to magically "take back" after the election is over. How can we expect such a deep, ugly, festering gash, ripping through our identity as a country, to instantly heal just because we've chosen a new president? What about the people on the other side? Do we believe that, after this personal, contentious battle that has stretched for over a year, they'll simply shrug their shoulders, forget everything that has happened, and move on? I find that highly unlikely.

This election has been far too personal and divisive precisely because we've forgotten how to disagree with one another, to debate the issues intelligently without going nuclear. We've thrown out the notion that you can "win" a political discussion without personally destroying your opponent in the process. We've gone directly to the nuclear option in American politics, without considering the consequences of that decision. Now, I wonder if there's any turning back to a time when elections were battle of ideas, not sensationalism. Now that we've hit the red button on our emotions and out-of-control behavior during an election year, have we set a new precedent for how we handle political debate and elections?

I'm already looking ahead four years to the next presidential election, and I'm concerned. Are we planning to go through all this again? Or, next time, will we resist the call to divisiveness? For that to happen, we need to start the healing now. We need to re-learn how to talk with each other, how to debate the issues intelligently, and how to avoid going nuclear every time we disagree with each other. Our vicious infighting is slowly tearing down the edifice our founding fathers built. The spirit of patriotism and working together toward a common goal is a flame that is flickering out, and as it fades, so does our unity. We need to set a better example, if only because of what's at stake here: our country, our image, and our reputation.

The world is watching. They are waiting to see if we can learn from this, or if we will keep repeating the same cycle of political embarrassment, over and over, ripping open the bloody scar time and time again until we've injured ourselves beyond the ability to heal. Much of the world still sees America as a superpower, a role model of democracy, humanity, and strength that they want to look up to and emulate. We cannot elevate the world, though, if our own house is in chaos. If we are divided as a country, we cannot help unite other countries behind ideas, causes, movements, and actions aimed at changing the world for the better.

NOVEMBER 9, 2016

The 45th President of the United States was elected last night. Many Americans woke up to what the media dubbed a "stunning upset." As is the case with most elections, some voters are celebrating while others are grieving; this is the inevitable nature of politics, especially in a country as large and diverse as America.

But why did this election feel so different? I believe it's because it was a defining moment for all of us as Americans. It tested who we are, our identity as a people, and our tolerance for one another. That's why I believe people are having such an emotional reaction to it.

But even in the midst of this volatile election story of extreme emotions and dramatically different perspectives as a country, we must find a way to keep our stories as individuals intact. No matter what is happening in Washington D.C., life still goes on and we all share one common value - our love for this country. That must always be kept in perspective.

For those of us who are parents, this idea of keeping a healthy perspective is even more amplified, because our children are looking to us to see how to react in the midst of heartfelt challenges. I will confess that I was one of the stunned and upset ones this morning. But I had to push my emotions aside. As a parent, my feelings had to be secondary to those of my child. I wanted to make sure to communicate the right message to Sofia about what she is now observing. This is what I wrote to her this morning.

Sofia, history has been made. And you are unique in that you have personally witnessed and felt it yourself. Cherish the memory and remember that the most important lesson we have learned from this election is to always respect someone else's point of view, even when it is opposite to yours. This has also reminded us that America is the greatest country in the world to allow all of its people to speak their minds in such a democratic way. But for us, we must continue to prove we are good women—intelligent, hard working, strong, proud of who and what we are—American Latina—and respectful. That's how we change the world one day at a time. I love you. So, be happy and proud, and when someone shares their excitement or sadness about this 2016 election, you smile and say, "I'm so happy to be an American."

Now, as you're reading this book, the 2016 election is in the history books. Fall gave way to winter and we are now entering the spring of 2017. Our country's newest presidency is in its infancy. None of us have any idea what the future holds, but if you take away just one thought from the book, I hope it will be this: We each hold the power to restore our American identity. Even as one single American, you are standing on the shoulders of greatness—of immigrants, of presidents, of soldiers who died for you, of civil rights leaders, of founding fathers and mothers, of inventors, of entrepreneurs, and of so many others.

The power we each hold extends so much further than a single vote cast every four years in a presidential election. Through our individual words and actions, and the examples we set as Americans every day in our lives and in our communities, we can help heal our collective wound. We can help our country come together again. We can help cure the cancer of racism; dispel the myths about newcomers; make people around us proud to call themselves American; and so much more. Together, we are Red, White, and Latina—Latino American, African American, Caucasian American, Asian American, European American, Hispanic American, Native American, Indian American, Arab American . . . We are collectively and equally Red, White, and Blue.

What would happen if we defied all expectations, came together as one country, and changed the conversation about one, unified American identity? Let's not wait four more years to do it. The clock starts now!

Real change never occurs from the top on down, [but] always from the bottom on up.

—Senator Bernie Sanders

REFERENCES & RESOURCES

CHAPTER 2

Fox25Boston.com. "Survivors outraged after learning Tsarnaev's family's trip to US paid for with American tax dollars." April 24, 2015. http://www.fox25boston.com/news/survivors-outraged-after-learning-tsarnaevs-familys-trip-to-us-paid-for-with-american-tax-dollars/143480567

NYDailyNews.com. "Angry mother of convicted Boston Marathon bomber Dzhokhar Tsarnaev says US 'will pay.'" April 10, 2015. http://www.nydailynews.com/news/crime/angry-mother-dzhokhar-tsarnaev-u-s-pay-article-1.2179362

RollingStone.com. "Jahar's World." July 17, 2013. http://www.rollingstone.com/culture/news/jahars-world-20130717

CHAPTER 3

Abc7.com. "UC Irvine student executive council vetoes US flag ban." March 7, 2015. http://abc7.com/education/uc-irvine-student-executive-council-vetoes-us-flag-ban/549279/

CHAPTER 4

Mtv.com. "Fifth Harmony's Camila pens powerful essay about growing up as an immigrant." September 15, 2016. http://www.mtv.com/news/2932652/camila-cabello-fifth-harmony-personal-essay-immigrant/

Butcher, Kristine F. and Morrison Piehl, Anne. "Why are Immigrants' Incarceration Rates so Low? Evidence of Selective Immigration, Deterrence, and Deportation." National Bureau of Economic Research. Working Paper Series. July 2007.

Politifact.com. "Steve Case says 40 percent of the Fortune 500 were started either by immigrants or children of immigrants." July 6, 2011. http://www.politifact.com/truth-o-meter/statements/2011/jul/06/steve-case/steve-case-says-40-percent-fortune-500-were-starte/

Phys.org. "One-third of US tech 'innovators' are immigrants: study." February 24, 2016. http://phys.org/news/2016-02-one-third-tech-immigrants.html

Kauffman.org. "The Economic Case for Welcoming Immigrant Entrepreneurs." September 8, 2015. http://www.kauffman.org/what-we-do/resources/entrepreneurship-policy-digest/the-economic-case-for-welcoming-immigrant-entrepreneurs

WashingtonPost.com. "This couple didn't tip their Latina server. They left a hateful message instead." August 21, 2016. https://www.washingtonpost.com/news/post-nation/wp/2016/08/21/

this-couple-didnt-tip-their-latina-server-they-left-a-hateful-message-instead/?utm_term=.f1eeb7fa5597

MigrationPolicy.org. "Frequently Requested Statistics on Immigrants and Immigration in the United States." April 14, 2016. http://www.migrationpolicy.org/article/frequently-requested-statistics-immigrants-and-immigration-united-states

Pbs.org. "They served their country. Now they can't live in it." September 10, 2015. http://www.pbs.org/newshour/updates/served-country-now-cant-live/

American Immigration Council. "Give The Facts a Fighting Chance." Special Report. December 2015.

Money.CNN.com. "5 immigration myths debunked." November 20, 2014. http://money.cnn.com/2014/11/20/news/economy/immigration-myths/

TheHill.com. "House rejects effort to ban illegal immigrants from military service." June 16, 2016. http://thehill.com/policy/finance/283762-house-rejects-effort-to-ban-illegal-immigrants-from-enlisting-in-military

MigrationPolicy.org. "Immigrants in the US Armed Forces." May 15, 2008. http://www.migrationpolicy.org/article/immigrants-us-armed-forces

ViceNews.com. "The Pentagon Will Allow Undocumented Immigrants to Join the US Military." September 26, 2014. https://news.vice.com/article/the-pentagon-will-allow-undocumented-immigrants-to-join-the-us-military

CCSF Oral History Project. "Myth 13: Today's Immigrants Are Not Learning English." June 2, 1015. https://ccsforalhistoryproject.wordpress.com/2015/06/02/myth-13-todays-immigrants-are-not-learning-English/

VoiceofAmerica.com. "Illegal US Immigrants Pay Billions in Taxes, But Is it Enough?" March 25, 2016. http://blogs.voanews. com/all-about-america/2016/03/25/illegal-us-immigrants-pay-billions-in-taxes-but-is-it-enough/

American Immigration Council (various reports); "How the United States Immigration System Works," "Why Don't They Just Get In Line? There Is No Line for Many Unauthorized Immigrants," "Did My Family Really Come "Legally"? Today's Immigration Laws Created a New Reality,"

CHAPTER 5

King Encycylopedia.Stanford.Edu. "25 March 1965. Address at the Conclusion of the Selma to Montgomery March." http:// kingencyclopedia.stanford.edu/encyclopedia/documentsentry/ doc_address_at_the_conclusion_of_selma_march.1.html

USNews.com. "Racist Fraternity Chant Learned During Leadership Cruise." March 27, 2015. http://www.usnews.com/news/ articles/2015/03/27/university-of-oklahoma-racist-chant-learned-during-leadership-cruise

Identities.Mic. "The US Army Has a Day Each Week When Racism is Allowed—What Could Possibly Go Wrong?" March 19, 2015. https://mic.com/articles/113310/why-the-u-s-army-doesn-t-need-racial-thursdays-a-special-day-for-racism#. KRrvk6Kb8

BuzzFeedNews.com. "Damage Caused During Baltimore Riots Estimated at $9 Million." May 13, 2015. https://www.buzzfeed. com/salvadorhernandez/damage-caused-during-baltimore-riots-estimated-at-9-million?utm_term=.uaNQAZdBk#. hgZ6D7pm1

Gawker.com. "Here's the Internal Memo from Starbucks' Disastrous Race-Relations Push." March 19, 2015. http://gawker.com/heres-the-internal-memo-from-starbucks-disastrous-race-1692472575

LATimes.com. "Starbucks stops writing 'Race Together' on cups." March 22, 2015. http://www.latimes.com/business/la-fi-starbucks-race-together-20150322-story.html

BaltimoreSun.com. "Baltimore police officers cleared in Freddie Gray case return to uncertain future." July 30, 2016. http://www.baltimoresun.com/news/maryland/freddie-gray/bs-md-officers-return-20160730-story.html

CHAPTER 7

UrbanConfessional.org. "How to Listen When You Disagree: A Lesson From the Republican National Convention." July 27, 2016. http://urbanconfessional.org/blog/howtodisagree

SanDiegoUnionTribune.com. "Hear a C-SPAN caller admit own racism, ask for help." August 24, 2016. http://www.sandiegouniontribune.com/sdut-cspan-caller-black-guest-how-to-be-less-prejudice-2016aug24-htmlstory.html

EPILOGUE

CBS SF Bay Area.com. "Survey Shows Voters Getting Stressed Out By Election 2016." October 18, 2016. http://sanfrancisco.cbslocal.com/2016/10/18/survey-shows-voters-getting-stressed-out-by-election-2016/

Morgan James
Speakers Group

↗ www.TheMorganJamesSpeakersGroup.com

We connect Morgan James published authors with live and online events and audiences whom will benefit from their expertise.

Morgan James makes all of our titles available
through the Library for All Charity Organization.

www.LibraryForAll.org